THE PRINCIPLED LEADER

A Common Sense Coaching And
Survival Guide For Leaders

Chuck Pledger

Copyright © 2019 by Chuck Pledger

All rights reserved. No part of this publication may be reproduced, distributed, or transmitted in any form or by any means, including photocopying, recording, or other electronic or mechanical methods, without the prior written permission of the author, except in the case of brief quotations embodied in critical reviews and certain other noncommercial uses permitted by copyright law.

◆ ◆ ◆

Text marked NIV are taken from THE HOLY BIBLE, NEW INTERNATIONAL VERSION®, NIV® Copyright © 1973, 1978, 1984, 2011 by Biblica, Inc.™ Used by permission. All rights reserved worldwide.

Text marked with GW: Scripture is taken from GOD'S WORD®, © 1995 God's Word to the Nations. Used by permission of Baker Publishing Group.

Text marked with PHILLIPS are taken from The New Testament in Modern English by J.B Phillips copyright © 1960, 1972 J. B. Phillips. Administered by The Archbishops' Council of the Church of England. Used by Permission.

Text marked CEB are taken from the Common English Bible® Copyright © 2010, 2011 by Common English Bible,™ Used by permission. All rights reserved worldwide, The "CEB" and "Common English Bible" trademarks are registered in the United States Patent and Trademark Office by Common English Bible. Use of either trademark requires the permission of Common English Bible.

CONTENTS

Title Page	
Copyright	
Introduction	2
How to use this book	4
Chapter 1 Fundamentals	5
Lesson 1: Vision	6
Lesson 2: Strategy and Planning	9
Lesson 3: Laser Focus	12
Lesson 4: Chief Protection Officer	15
Lesson 5: Ultimate Purpose	18
Chapter 2 Personal Attributes	21
Lesson 6: Integrity	22
Lesson 7: Always Positive	25
Lesson 8: Humbleness	28
Lesson 9: Consistent Temperament	31
Lesson 10: Gratitude	34
Lesson 11: Passion	37
Lesson 12: Insatiably Curious	40
Lesson 13: Accountable	43
Lesson 14: Dedication	46
Lesson 15: Counselor	49
Lesson 16: Sense of Humor	52
Lesson 17: Love and Caring	55
Lesson 18: Generous	58

Lesson 19: Diligence	61
Lesson 20: Faith	64
Chapter 3 Best Practices	67
Lesson 21: Gratitude Over Criticism	68
Lesson 22: Mentoring	71
Lesson 23: Open Communication	74
Lesson 24: Setbacks are Opportunities	77
Lesson 25: The Golden Rule	80
Lesson 26: Senseless Worry	83
Lesson 27: Fair and Just	86
Lesson 28: Service Oriented	89
Lesson 29: Professional Family	92
Lesson 30: Allow for failure	95
Lesson 31: Encouraging Words	98
Lesson 32: Sharpening Iron	101
Lesson 33: Mindset of the Team	104
Lesson 34: Balance versus Harmony	107
Lesson 35: Behavior Problems	110
Lesson 36: Lack of Performance	113
Lesson 37: Hiring the Right Team	116
Lesson 38: Maturing Leaders	120
Lesson 39: Positive Culture	123
Lesson 40: Diversity	126
Lesson 41: Delegation	129
Lesson 42: Perfection or Results	132
Lesson 43: Molehills or Mountains	135
Wrapping things up	138
About the author	140

INTRODUCTION

In 2004, I was laying in the intensive care unit early in the morning on Mother's Day. I heard the doctor tell the nurse in the hall after he examined me, "You need to call the family in, as soon as possible." I had bacterial meningitis, an infection of the fluid around the spinal cord that had reached my brain. The infection was the result of a series of complications after back surgery for a herniated disk. I remember not being able to move or respond but I could clearly hear what was being said around me and understood the urgency of the caregiver's concerns.

This single traumatic event had a dramatic impact on how I view life now and what is most important to me professionally, personally, and spiritually. It had a profound effect on my leadership philosophy and how I manage people, projects, events, and challenges. This experience intensified my commitment to my life mission, which is to inspire and positively impact the lives of those around me.

This book is for people in authority, leaders, and

those looking to move into a leadership role. It is based upon real life business situations that I have experienced throughout my career. I would love to say I am an expert and that I follow my own advice all the time but that simply would not be true. The reason I feel so strongly about sharing these principles and personal attributes is that I've failed or witnessed someone else fail in each of these areas. I want you to learn from these mistakes and be inspired to become the best leader possible; a leader with value based principles built upon your personal beliefs.

    I've noticed when we face an overwhelming challenge that most people turn to the core of their value system. For me that is my faith. Although this is not a "religious" book, I find that all the principles are drawn from my faith based beliefs, values, and upbringing. To that end, I have included bible references in each lesson to highlight the deep core values in my personal journey of leadership. Your experience is likely very different than mine. I would urge you to explore, understand, and tap into your own values and core beliefs as you study these principles. You will find they are tightly connected.

HOW TO USE THIS BOOK

This book is intended to be used as a personal coach and mentor to guide you through leadership concepts. It will teach you how to be a leader versus a person in the position of authority. Each lesson touches on a basic principle or personal attribute for you to consider and ends with questions for reflection to help internalize the material.

It can also be used as a reference or survival guide to help you through challenges as they arise over time. The book is divided into leadership topics that can be reviewed and put into practice at any time you find yourself struggling with a situation.

CHAPTER 1
FUNDAMENTALS

The first lessons are what I call the fundamentals of leadership. These principles represent characteristics and practices that are paramount to a leader's success. If you do nothing else, focus on these five fundamental leadership capabilities and you will be ahead of most leaders.

LESSON 1: VISION

Proverbs 29:18 (CEB) When there's no vision, the people get out of control, but whoever obeys instruction is happy.

Only a leader with a powerful and passionate vision can inspire a team to accomplish the impossible.

An inspiring vision can literally change the world. Think back to famous speeches that created a vision such as John F. Kennedy's inauguration where he stated, "Ask not what your country can do for you—ask what you can do for your country." Martin Luther King, Jr. delivered the "I have a dream" speech that equally impacted the nation. Nelson Mandela spent 20 years in jail for opposing apartheid after he delivered the speech at his trial where he stated, "it is an ideal for which I am prepared to die."

Jesus' final words to his apostles provided a vision that transformed them from cowering and defeated men hiding in a back room to leaders who would spend the rest of their lives committed to a vision set before them. How was it possible to turn these men around in such a short amount of time? It's simple. They believed in a vision.

Granted, we are not likely leading a team of apostles or a revolution but a life impacting vision is still critical. This is why I have it listed as the first fundamental role of the leader. One cannot inspire a team to greatness without a clear and impactful vision. A vision paints the picture of a highly desirable state we wish to attain. It is a calling to those dedicated to the vision rather than a mandate or job. Those that are "called" will passionately go to the ends of the earth to attain the vision. The impact our team will make is highly related to the inspiration set forth in the vision.

We are naturally attracted to a leader who has a vision and a plan. It is the leader's vision coupled with each individual's passion that motivates and inspires an individual to work harder and longer in order to accomplish a goal. Paychecks, rewards, and recognition are important but a vision is what will truly inspire a team to greatness.

My wife and I have volunteered at many homeless shelters over the years. The ones that succeed and profoundly impact their local communities are the ones that have a vision that grabs the heart and compels us to action. It takes an impactful vision to move a person beyond simply making a donation and actually getting personally involved. There is an organization where I live called the Columbus Dream Center that inspires an army of volunteers to care for and give hope and dreams to those that are struggling. Their vision is seen in the name...Dream Center. Their mission is simple: Find a need and meet it. Find a hurt and heal it. Those that passionately volunteer are impacted and blessed as much as those they are serving.

Your team will only accomplish great and unimaginable things when they have bought into your vision as a leader. They must believe in what they are doing and why they are doing it. Most people don't want to just have a job or punch a clock; they want to know they are making an impact. A passionate, heartfelt vision provides the reason and drive for us to work and gives meaning to the work we do. A team will be fully engaged and motivated when their hearts are engaged. They will not only impact the lives of others through their efforts but will also be deeply moved themselves.

Questions for reflection:

1. Does my vision motivate and inspire my team?
2. Does it support the mission of the organization?

LESSON 2: STRATEGY AND PLANNING

Jeremiah 29:11 (NIV) For I know the plans I have for you, declares the Lord, plans to prosper you and not to harm you, plans to give you hope and a future.

Without planning and strategy, a vision is little more than a dream that will never be accomplished.

A vision is worthless without a plan. An organization without a strategy is similar to a team of peewee soccer players. The kids are all running after the ball regardless of their position. They kick it often with no particular direction in mind. Others are sitting on the field distracted by everything. There is little forward motion of the ball. Regardless of how passionate our team may be about a vision, they will work against each other and fail miserably unless there is a clearly defined strategy that is continually reviewed and communicated frequently.

I've worked with many cyber security startups over the years. All too frequently, the leadership teams tell me that if I will simply get them in front of the chief security officer that they will convince them to use their solution. This rarely works and is not sustainable. Many of these companies have tremendous vision and passion but there is no plan. Launching a new solution requires a well thought out sales and marketing strategy.

I've watched many startups hire dozens of sales people with no other strategy than to knock on as many doors as possible. They were hired primarily for their contacts. Within six months or so they are back to square one and replacing the sales team because, "they obviously don't know how to sell". In fact, one startup where I was engaged was on their fourth sales team makeover in just over two years. This is the definition of insanity! The management team completely ignored the basics of leadership. They had a good vision but they will never execute on it because their de facto strategy was to keep blaming the sales team for lack of results.

When vision and strategy come together, the stage is set for great things to happen. Vision naturally inspires passion and urgency. The strategy defines the roadmap so that everyone is pulling the same direction at the same time. John F. Kennedy inspired the nation to land on the moon in a speech in 1961. He quickly expanded the space program and NASA put together a plan. In 1969, eight short years later, Neil Armstrong became the first man to walk on the moon. I can still vividly remember watching the flag being planted on the moon on live TV. This would have never happened without a strategy that mapped out the path forward.

I've seen and experienced equally phenomenal results in a business setting. For example, my team experienced meager results initially after we sold the startup where I was running sales. It wasn't until we completely reworked the vision and the strategy for selling the solution that we began to see significant traction with our parent company. Over the next four years, the team experienced 2500% growth. That is the power of combing vision with strategy. The magic can only happen when the two are combined.

Questions for reflection:

1. Do you have a well-documented strategy that has clearly defined objectives, owners, measurable results, and time frames?
2. Do each of your team members have a similar strategy that supports the overall strategy?
3. Do you review the plan, risks, and results on a regular basis?

LESSON 3: LASER FOCUS

Proverbs 4:25-27 (NIV) Let your eyes look straight ahead; fix your gaze directly before you. Give careful thought to the paths for your feet and be steadfast in all your ways. Do not turn to the right or the left; keep your foot from evil.

Relentless laser-like focus on the strategy must start with the leader and be driven with a sense of urgency to every team member.

It is the leader's job to provide vision that instills passion, develop plans, and continuously maintain a determined focus on the objectives. I've watched many teams move mountains and overcome insurmountable obstacles in record time when they have all three.

Companies often have self-inflicted wounds. One that I frequently see is what I call the trap of chasing shiny objects. "The potential marquee customer will buy the solution immediately if we just add this one feature." The only problem is the feature will require months to develop with significant costs impacting the existing roadmap, and dramatically shortening the time before it becomes necessary to acquire additional funding. Like a fish that strikes a lure sparkling in the sun, companies that are not focused on their objectives and strategy will fall for these traps. The executives are so enthralled that they might be able to land the big fish that they abandon their well thought out plan, assuming there was one.

Years ago, I was at a startup focused on telecommunication companies. Our solution could be used as a long distance switching solution or as a local exchange switch to provide features to subscribers. The roadmap would shift wildly between the two extremes based on the requirements of the most recent opportunity. Obviously, the company never gained traction and eventually sold the intellectual property at a tremendous loss for the investors.

It is easy for even the most disciplined organizations to lose focus or get sidetracked. Chasing shiny objects, skunk-work projects, personnel distractions, or straying from the plan can all have significant and costly consequences. They hinder our ability as a leader to accomplish our strategy and vision. These types of projects should be included in the organizational strategy if they are necessary for driving innovation. The point is that the plan should not change constantly.

Think of this like a game of tug of war. When the team is not focused, there is a huge amount of energy expended but very little forward progress because everyone is pulling against each other. Imagine what could be accomplished if the entire team was laser focused and pulling in the same direction. In the example above, the company would have been far better served if they validated the market need, picked a specific direction, and sent the sales team out with a singular focus. Instead, they tried to be all things to all people with no focus and as a result failed.

Another challenge I see is that many leaders often confuse activity with results. For example, the team had 25 sales calls this week. The developers generated 50,000 lines of code. Both statements are meaningless unless they produce results. Focusing on the right activity produces consistent and repeatable results.

Questions for reflection:
1. Identify team activities that distract or hinder progress for producing results.
2. How do you actively communicate the strategy and measure the team's results?

LESSON 4: CHIEF PROTECTION OFFICER

John 17:12a (NIV) While I was with them, I protected them and kept them safe by that name you gave me.

A*team will only perform at the highest levels of success when they know their leader has their back.*

I received a call late in the afternoon telling me I had to eliminate half my team because of mandatory reductions in spite of the fact we were the fastest growing and highest margin contributor in the organization. I was given the names of those who had been chosen. Included in the list was one of my sales engineers. He had been dealing with serious health issues for some time. He informed me just that morning that his mother had passed away suddenly. I could not in good conscious let him go at this point and was able to get an extension. I helped him find another role in the company before I was forced to downsize him. He continued to be a friend and an asset to me even in his new role throughout the years.

As leaders, we must protect and fight for our teams as if they were our family. Our employees are not resources or numbers but rather, our most important investments. They are our friends and the ones that will ultimately enable our success. You will develop an unbreakable loyalty, trust, and respect among your team when they see you go to battle and contend for them. They will in turn fight for you even in the most difficult of circumstances and help you move mountains in order to achieve your objectives.

I was not able to save all the people on my team during that or subsequent rounds of cuts but I continued to fight for them. I reached out to my friends both inside and outside of the company to help find them new jobs. I was a reference for each one of them. To this day, I still consider them trusted friends and chat with many of them on a regular basis.

Another startup I was at had an entire team of people at a large trade show in San Diego. After a long day on the floor, a group of us headed out to the

Gaslamp Quarter for a late dinner with some of our resellers and didn't finish until around 11:30 PM. Most of the team decided to head to the bars for a nightcap while a few of us headed back to the hotel. I made a point to my team that they needed to be at their post on time and ready to go the next morning. As we walked back to the hotel, one of the guys pointed out that his dad, a very successful CEO, always told him, "Nothing good ever happens after midnight." Those words certainly rang true in that situation. I've shared this advice on many occasions with many different people.

The next morning, the entire executive team was in the booth as some of my team stumbled in clearly still inebriated having stayed up much of the night. I quickly sent them out and covered for them but it didn't go without notice. That incident cost me a tremendous amount of political capital with the leadership team; more importantly, it gained the trust and respect of my team for protecting them during their lapse of judgment. Needless to say, it never happened again. We have laughed about this over the years but it certainly was a painful learning experience for all of us at that time.

Questions for reflection:
1. Recall specific actions you have taken to protect members of your team.
2. Did those actions produce the desired results?
3. What would you do differently?

LESSON 5: ULTIMATE PURPOSE

Proverbs 19:21 (NIV) Many are the plans in a person's heart, but it is the Lord's purpose that prevails.

Like a rope made of many strands, an organization is strongest when the vision and strategy of every individual team is highly supportive of the organization's objectives.

The only reason we have a leadership role is to advance the objectives of our organization. Our vision, planning, and focus must align with these corporate objectives.

When I start in a leadership or consulting role

with a new company, the very first thing I do is begin to understand the company objectives, expectations, and challenges. I then build a business strategy around those three key topics and define success metrics to know that I am accomplishing what I need to get done.

As the verse above states, I may have a long list of personal plans or goals that I would like to accomplish but it is ultimately the organization's purpose that must prevail. If our plan doesn't prioritize and accomplish the organizational goals, then our employment will be very brief. Every goal and objective we develop for our team must support the corporate strategy.

What happens if our personal purpose is different from that of the employer? It creates a very difficult and potentially hostile environment in which to work. It may be a matter of integrity and personal ethics. I have a good friend that is an excellent sales person. He was in a meeting with a long time customer and a senior executive of the new startup he had recently joined. The executive not only stretched the truth, he completely lied about their customer base and the accounts that had purchased their solution. My friend's purpose was to win accounts with integrity and trust in order to earn the right to continually do business with them in the future. This particular customer was a personal friend that he had worked with for years and he did not want to tarnish his relationship. After the meeting he confronted the executive and was told to do or say whatever it takes to close a deal because, "That's how deals get done." The company's purpose related to sales was directly opposed to my friend's purpose and moral integrity. His purpose and method of selling was never going to align with that of the company. It was not long after that he moved on to another company.

It's critical going into a new role to understand the purpose and expectations in order to be able to accomplish the objectives. It's equally important to revisit these goals and expectations on a regular basis to ensure that we remain focused on the highest priorities of the company.

When we deliver on the company objectives and provide a positive impact on the purpose and vision, we will more than likely ensure that our team has value, receives increased funding and headcount, and avoids mandatory cuts. In other words, delivering on the company purpose will earn clout or "silver bullets" that can be used at a later time.

Questions for reflection:

1. Prioritize and document your understanding of the team's objectives and expectations.
2. Validate these with your management and those impacted by your team's efforts.
3. If they don't align, then adjust your plan.

CHAPTER 2
PERSONAL ATTRIBUTES

The lessons in this section describe the core values and personal attributes of leaders. These characteristics are the outward expression of our individual personal belief system. Personal attributes are what give leaders a strong foundation.

LESSON 6: INTEGRITY

Proverbs 11:3 (NIV) The integrity of the upright guides them, but the unfaithful are destroyed by their duplicity.

Integrity takes a lifetime to build and seconds to destroy. Guard it at all costs.

Integrity is about being honest, having strong moral principles along with the conviction and fortitude to be true to those principles, and doing the right thing even when no one is watching. To me, integrity is the most important personal attribute and must be protected.

Think of integrity like a balance scale. On one side are our positive actions that build up our integrity. On the other side are the things that tear down our integrity. The problem is that the balance isn't centered.

It takes much more positive effort to overcome just a little bit of negative activity. Any action that negatively impacts our integrity seems to be magnified by orders of magnitude.

Integrity is not compartmentalized or bound to a specific area of our lives. Things we do in our personal life have an impact on our professional lives. I suspect we all know someone that has had an affair or cheated on a significant other. That is definitely a personal event. Does the fact that they are cheating on their spouse impact your perception of their integrity? It obviously depends greatly on the situation but on the surface, their actions tell you that they have no problem deceiving or hurting another person for self-gratification. Why would we believe it would be any different in the work environment given a similar set of circumstances?

I've heard many people justify their acts of indulgence or discretion by stating something like, "What happens in Vegas stays in Vegas" or "If it happens outside of the outer belt, then it doesn't count." Integrity is as much about what we do in private when people aren't watching as it is about what is seen publicly. Wrong or hurtful actions aren't justified because they were done in private. Integrity is more about who we are than what we do.

I expect and encourage integrity from my team. More importantly, I expect integrity from myself. If I'm not living my life professionally and personally within a given set of moral principles it will show up in the way I conduct myself. My team and friends will stop trusting me and lose respect for me no matter what great things I may have accomplished in the past. We can't lead without integrity.

Integrity comes from deep within and is the outward expression that flows from our belief system. It is our moral compass that always provides direction and points to True North. For some, this belief system is rooted in their faith or a belief in a higher power. For others, it's based on life experience. Either way, our integrity is based on this set of beliefs formulated into a personal code of ethics that we are compelled to follow.

We are all going to make mistakes that impact our integrity. No one is perfect. How can we recover? The very first thing to do is acknowledge our mistake and apologize to the person we hurt as soon as possible. Most people will forgive but don't expect them to forget. It will still take time for them to fully trust you. That's just human nature. It will take time and many positive affirmations before they fully trust you again. Think back to the off centered scale where we started. It takes far more positive effort to balance out the negative impact to our integrity.

Questions for reflection:
1. Write out a list of the things that you view as essential characteristics of integrity.
2. How true and faithful are you to this list?

LESSON 7: ALWAYS POSITIVE

Philippians 4:8 (NIV) Finally, brothers and sisters, whatever is true, whatever is noble, whatever is right, whatever is pure, whatever is lovely, whatever is admirable—if anything is excellent or praiseworthy—think about such things.

*positive attitude is a choice we must make.*

It is important for leaders to have a positive attitude. We face a myriad of tough choices, events, and circumstances that seem to come out of nowhere to entangle and derail us. If we don't choose to be positive, we will be quickly dragged down and overwhelmed.

I have a few friends that are miserable to be around in the best of circumstances. They view the world through storm colored glasses where the sky is always gray and raining. I tend to avoid them because I don't want to be dragged down by their negative attitudes. Think about our teams. How motivated will they be if we are always in a foul, miserable mood?

Our attitude is a choice rather than the result of our circumstances. We can choose to be positive and assume the best things are going to happen to us or we can be Chicken Little and view the world as if the sky is falling. I firmly believe that when we choose to be positive, good things will happen even during the most difficult of circumstances. Positive people attract positive results while negative people attract negative results.

It's not always easy to be positive. It takes effort and practice. By nature most of us tend to worry about our situation. I'm not saying that we should ignore the challenges but the way we view them creates a self-fulfilling prophecy. The verse above is a prime example of how to practice being positive. It's simple in theory but sometimes hard to do in practice.

For me, I always start out my day with something positive. For years, I would turn the news on while I made breakfast. I was instantly inundated with negative political, social, and world problems. Now, I find something positive to read and meditate on before I start my day. I focus on the things that are true, noble, right, pure, excellent, and praiseworthy. By doing this, it changes my entire perspective for the upcoming day. I do the same as I go to bed each night. I don't want to spend the night tossing, turning, and worrying about problems. I focus on the things that made a positive impact.

There is much more to being positive than how we start and end our day. We need to look at every situation from a positive perspective. I have a good friend that always says, "It's never as good as it seems or as bad as it seems." There is a lot of wisdom in that statement and I have found it to be true in most circumstances. When a difficult situation arises, I always try to find a positive outcome or at least something for which I can be grateful. Even rephrasing a negative outcome to a positive statement can be beneficial such as the famous quote ascribed to Thomas Edison. "I have not failed. I've just found 10,000 ways that won't work."

When I was young, I was always told to look for the silver lining in every situation. There is always something positive that can be found. The best thing about being positive is that those around us will typically reflect our attitude. Positive attitudes generate positive results.

Questions for reflection:
1. What actions have you taken this week to focus on having a positive outlook?
2. Are there areas for improvement?

LESSON 8: HUMBLENESS

Numbers 12:3 (NIV) Now Moses was a very humble man, more humble than anyone else on the face of the earth.

James 4:6b (NIV) That is why Scripture says: "God opposes the proud but shows favor to the humble."

*A**n egotistical person in a position of authority will demand respect but a humble leader earns it.*

The story of Moses is an interesting example of humility. Moses was born into slavery, raised by the Pharaoh's daughter in Egypt, murdered an Egyptian soldier, fled Egypt, and led the Jewish people out of captivity. God permitted Moses to be in his presence on a regular basis. Moses had every right to be proud and arrogant but he was just the opposite.

Throughout the bible there is an emphasis on humility and how God favors the humble and opposes the proud. Many of the leaders in the bible all seemed to come from lowly, unpretentious backgrounds: Abraham, Moses, King David, Jesus, the apostles, and many others. From my experience, it is easier to work with the person who is humble and open than the person that is proud and feels they know all the answers.

A person that is proud, egotistical, and arrogant typically feels that they have gained their position of power through their own efforts and strength. They know everything and to seek advice or counsel would be seen as a sign of weakness. Of the leaders I know that fit into this category, very few of them are able to take criticism or advice from others because it doesn't fit their narrative. They need to be seen as the person who knows all the answers and isn't dependent upon anyone else. Many of them are in fact very smart, talented, and capable people but their pride can become an obstacle.

Humble leaders seem to appreciate the boundaries of their abilities and are not afraid to ask questions to produce the best results. They often feel like they rose to a level of authority in spite of themselves. A common misconception is that a humble person is weak and cannot command authority in a cutthroat world. My experience has been just the opposite. Humbleness is extreme power under control. A humble leader will earn the respect of others by their actions where a proud leader will talk about the great things they have done and either expect or demand to be respected.

I've worked with and for many managers that fall into both camps. The reality is that both can accomplish the job and produce results. The real question is if one style is better than the other. In my opinion, a humble leader has the ability to pull the team together through a more collaborative approach where everyone is brought into the decision making process producing a much better result. Their employees love and respect them. An egotistical leader will typically proclaim, "This is what we are doing. Get on board or move out of the way." They demand loyalty and as a result often have a high turnover rate.

There are certainly times where I needed to rely on my title or ego in order to produce results. I've had employees defiantly resist change to the point I gave them an option to get on board with my program or leave. My preference is to lean towards being the humble but confident leader.

Questions for reflection:
1. What type of leader are you?
2. Does your leadership style produce the necessary results?

LESSON 9: CONSISTENT TEMPERAMENT

Proverbs 29:11 (NIV) Fools give full vent to their rage, but the wise bring calm in the end.

A leader's consistent temperament is paramount to a highly effective work environment.

The leader of the team will typically set the temperament for the work environment. Leaders who let their emotions swing across a wide spectrum with frequent outbursts will create a chaotic and impulsive environment. I've seen displays of anger, over reaction, or vindictiveness destroy teams and entire organizations. The team will walk on eggshells not knowing what to expect at any given moment. I've been a part of many teams like this and it is never a fun environment.

To make matters worse, when the leader has an uncontrolled outburst, those emotions transfer to the entire team like an uncontrolled wildfire. Good decision-making is almost always compromised because of the elevated emotions. Relationships and trust are often damaged sometimes beyond repair. Productivity will be low and turnover high.

There are times when a strong outward emotion or anger is an appropriate response to a situation but it is rare. For example, anger might be the catalyst that motivates a person to take action. The challenge is controlling the response. My brother had a roommate in college that was an engineering student. He was a very smart guy but apparently didn't have much common sense. He placed an unopened can of ravioli on the stove to warm it up. A few minutes later, it exploded covering the kitchen in ravioli and shrapnel. That is often the result of uncontrolled anger. There can be a lot of collateral damage and more often than not, it makes a huge mess.

I received a scathing voicemail from a member of my sales team regarding a particular matter that was a concern to him. I forwarded the message to a couple other members of the executive team including the CEO to get clarification before I returned the call. I was told to immediately fire the person because of the inappropriateness of the call, the employee's tone, and obvious lack of respect.

I took a different approach. I called the employee back once I had the necessary information. Instead of blowing up, having my ego bent out of shape because a person yelled at me, and taking an immediate action to fire him, I remained calm. There had in fact been a mistake that impacted him so the issue was justified although his tone was way out of line. I had known him for a long time and this was out of character for him. We solved the problem in a matter of minutes and spent the remainder of time talking about what was behind the emotional outburst.

Had I acted rashly out of anger and not taken the time to listen, I would have fired my friend that day. I probably would have been justified in doing so but that wasn't the best course of action for either us. As a leader, we must maintain a consistent temperament in order to make clear and reasonable decisions when we are surrounded by chaos.

Questions for reflection:
1. Do you find that you manage out of anger and by instilling fear?
2. The next time you sense you are going to lash out in anger, take a deep breath, and pause until you understand all sides of the story. Then react calmly with control.

LESSON 10: GRATITUDE

1 Thessalonians 5:16-18 (NIV) Rejoice always, pray continually, give thanks in all circumstances; for this is God's will for you in Christ Jesus.

Success is a team sport. No one ever succeeds without help from others.

I believe gratitude is the opposite of ego. It is a matter of personal pronouns. The person with a large ego focuses on "I" whereas the person full of gratitude focuses on "You". Every person that has risen to the top of the organizational chart or become a person of power, influence, and authority has only done so through the help of others. There are no exceptions to this rule. Leaders must never forget or take this for granted.

I was focused on a specific customer for part of my career in sales. I was well connected with the leadership and staff at this particular customer. The VP of Sales from an upcoming startup approached me and offered me a position, stock options, increased salary, and title. Soon after I started, I quickly realized I was hired only for my contacts. Once I introduced the VP of Sales to my contacts and helped him build a relationship, my value to the startup declined substantially.

This manager would typically use the phrase, "I accomplished this" when referring to any customer of importance and never acknowledged the fact that it was his team that set the ground work, built the rapport, identified the needs, and set up the meetings. He took sole credit. He is the type of leader that I call a "Leech". He takes from people as long as they have something he needs. He is the type of person that rises to the top by stepping on people on the way up while taking all the credit.

As another example, I know a CEO that sold a very successful company and personally made hundreds of millions of dollars. He then invested into a new company. Not a single person from his former company chose to come with him even after any contractual non-compete clause had expired. This is a pretty good indicator that he used people and tossed them aside when he no longer needed them. There was no loyalty to him.

There is another type of person that rises to the top that believes success is a team sport. I had a former manager tell me, "I can't be successful until I make everyone on my team successful." This type of leader is full of gratitude. It doesn't mean they are any less demanding or successful. The difference is in the path they take to get to the top. The grateful leader pulls his team along with him being outwardly grateful to each person. They win and lose together.

At the end of the day, I've seen both types of people be extremely successful in their endeavors. One will leave behind a trail of used and ungrateful employees that helped him reach his goal but were thrown aside. The grateful leader will reach the top and have an army of people dedicated and willing to help him get to yet the next level of success.

I believe the real difference in these two types of leaders has to do with selfishness. One person is solely focused on personal gain while the other is selfless and has a desire to see each person succeed. I suspect most leaders vary in the middle of these two extremes.

Questions for reflection:

1. What style of leadership do you tend to gravitate towards - Selfless or selfish?
2. Are you comfortable where you are? If not, what steps can you take to move more to one side or the other?

LESSON 11: PASSION

Matthew 6:20-21 (GW) Instead, store up treasures for yourselves in heaven, where moths and rust don't destroy and thieves don't break in and steal. Your heart will be where your treasure is.

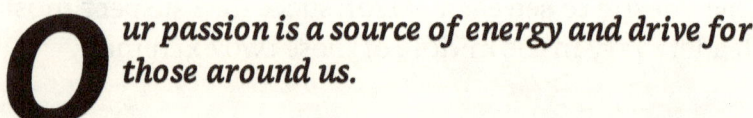

O*ur passion is a source of energy and drive for those around us.*

I view passion as any compelling emotion or strong feeling that drives one to action. Love and jealousy are obvious examples but it takes on a different characteristic for a leader. Passion isn't typically focused on another individual but rather an objective or purpose. It is the rocket fuel that ignites our ambition to accomplish something extraordinary. It drives us to relentlessly pursue a dream. When we are passionate, we find ways around, through, or over roadblocks that would stop any rational person.

Passion is driven by emotion. It is the thing that we long for the most, our greatest treasure. I love the words in the verse above. Your heart will be where your treasure is. What is unfortunate is that most people never find what they are truly passionate about. They don't find that treasure to pursue that touches and moves their heart. They are simply drifting in an ocean being pushed here and there.

I began to understand my life mission once I faced the reality that I might die lying in a hospital bed because of bacterial meningitis without ever accomplishing anything of lasting importance. My desire is to inspire and positively impact as many lives as possible. It is my reason for writing this book. I don't want anyone to get to the end of their life wonder if they made an impact and lived life to the fullest. I want to inspire you to live a life worth living so that you can also make a positive difference for everyone you meet.

I know a lot of people that are fanatical about a sports team. I live in Columbus, Ohio. The Ohio State Buckeye's Football team is an obsession for many people here in town. Many are also enthusiastic about the Cleveland Browns; their fans never give up hope. What I have never understood is how a person can have that much passion for a team but not have an even greater calling for something that is truly important or inspirational to them.

I've interviewed many people over the course of

my career. I'll often ask them about their passion. I usually get the typical interview type of answers about career, financial gain, or sometimes family. It's rare that I will find someone that wants to change the world. That's the person I want to hire. It's easier to guide someone that is driven than it is to get a person to move from a standstill.

A person with true passion is contagious likely because they are so rare. When a person is truly called to a particular cause, others see the unique quality and are inclined to follow. I have a friend that runs a non-profit called Orphan World Relief. His true love is obvious the moment you meet him because of his passion. He has inspired countless others to join him in his cause. He is relentlessly focused. This is the kind of calling that moves mountains. This is the kind of passion that leaders should aspire to have.

Questions for reflection:
1. What is your passion?
2. Where is your "treasure" for that's where your heart will be?
3. Is your passion self-centered or is it one that others will be inspired to follow?

LESSON 12: INSATIABLY CURIOUS

Matthew 7:7-8 (NIV) "Ask and it will be given to you; seek and you will find; knock and the door will be opened to you. For everyone who asks receives; the one who seeks finds; and to the one who knocks, the door will be opened."

Never stop learning or you will quickly become irrelevant.

In order to stay relevant in our field or to move into a new field we must continually educate and push ourselves. This is true for everyone but especially leaders since they set the overall tone for the team.

I've worked with many leaders that are still using

the same tired techniques they used twenty or thirty years ago. There are definitely principles of management and leadership that are evergreen, many of which I discuss in this book. We still must continually educate ourselves because so much has changed. Millennials, for example, need to be motivated, coached, and managed entirely different than a person that is fifty years old.

As an example, I have a good friend that has a degree in engineering. He works in the utilities industry on the emergency response team. He puts in his hours and leaves. He doesn't seem to care about advances in his career or continually increasing his income. He has no desire to put in countless hours at work. He simply wants to make enough money to enable him to sky dive, rock climb, and travel.

Being an effective leader means, we devote time to learning activities that help us improve. One of the leaders I've always admired was insatiably curious. He was an avid reader. In fact, he would frequently read while walking on a treadmill. He would read fiction, non-fiction, self-help, articles, or anything to increase his knowledge. He could have an in depth discussion on just about any topic.

I spend countless hours observing, interviewing and questioning other leaders about their best practices and what works for them. I'm always curious about how to improve my skills and the skills of my team. Observing how others lead provides a tremendous amount of knowledge. It is the practical application of this knowledge that over time develops into true insight and wisdom.

I also feel it is critical to learn about things outside of our career domain. I am always studying or learning something new. I grew up playing guitar. In my late forties, I decided that I would learn to play bass, piano, and drums. I spent the last two years learning to rock climb, which is as much of a mental exercise as it is physical. I taught myself how to build wood furniture out of reclaimed barn wood. I learned to design and build websites, write visual basic code, and leverage social networking in marketing campaigns. I didn't do these because it was necessary for my career. Rather, I did them because they stimulated my mind.

I think part of the reason so many leaders don't progress is that they stop learning and challenging themselves. If we continue to "ask, seek, and knock", we will find many doors opened to us that we never thought possible.

Questions for reflection:

1. When was the last time you purposely focused on learning something new completely outside of your career?

LESSON 13: ACCOUNTABLE

Romans 14:12 (NIV) So then, each of us will give an account of ourselves to God.

A leader must always be accountable for the actions of their team without placing blame.

The most successful leaders that I know take responsibility for the actions of their teams, regardless of the outcome. They don't blame the team when something doesn't go according to plan. In contrast, they give the team credit when things go exceptionally well.

The true colors of the leadership team are usually revealed once a company launches their product and immediately run into resistance as they attempt to sell the solution. A significant amount of cash is flowing out of the door with little or no immediate return. The CFO begins to highlight the cash burn rate. The sales team begins to point to the lack of leads being developed from marketing. Marketing pushes back on the effectiveness of the sales people. Meanwhile, there is a large inventory of stock that is aging in a warehouse. Events compound quickly and it is easy for everyone to point fingers.

The companies that I have seen excel are those where the leaders are accountable for their actions and hold their coworkers accountable without pointing fingers. There is a big difference in holding another team accountable and blaming them for your failure.

For example, a sales leader should build their go to market strategy on a set of assumptions. Those assumptions may include input from other parts of the organization such as marketing. It is my responsibility as a sales leader to identify those expectations that drive my assumptions. I might build a model that requires an input of 10 leads per day from marketing. The leadership team must agree on the joint plan, which clearly indicates the point of demarcation and deliverables. I'm no longer pointing fingers and blaming someone else if marketing doesn't deliver. As a leadership team, we can measure the results and understand what to fix when the expectations are clearly delineated. This is obviously an oversimplified example but it drives the point that leaders need to be accountable for what they control and ensure that their coworkers are also accountable without pointing fingers. "Friendly fire" and blame doesn't help anyone.

I've also witnessed many managers blame someone on his team when the desired results were not achieved. "I assigned that project to Bob and he dropped the ball." "John wasn't able to close the deal before quarter end so we missed the number." In my mind, there is nothing worse than a manager like this. I won't even call these people leaders because they are missing many of the basic skills necessary to lead. They are naïve in thinking that blaming others will take the pressure off of them.

An effective leader must be accountable. "We missed the number because I didn't accurately qualify several deals and they slipped." This statement squarely puts the blame on my shoulders because I failed to manage the team or didn't forecast properly. "The project failed because I didn't manage the project owner." These are examples of a leader being accountable. If I were presenting these types of results, I would also include an action plan to ensure that it doesn't happen again.

Questions for reflection:

1. Recall some examples where you passed the blame to another part of the organization or a team member.
2. What were the results and what would have been a better way to handle the situation?

LESSON 14: DEDICATION

Daniel 3:17-18 (NIV) If we are thrown into the blazing furnace, the God we serve is able to deliver us from it, and he will deliver us from Your Majesty's hand. But even if he does not, we want you to know, Your Majesty, that we will not serve your gods or worship the image of gold you have set up."

 *person's dedication will be in direct proportion to their belief in their vision.*

The story above is about Shadrach, Meshach, and Abednego. They were Jewish captives exiled to Babylon. King Nebuchadnezzar created a ninety-foot tall golden image that everyone was mandated to bow before and worship. The three men refused knowing it might cost them their lives. They were dedicated to their faith to the point of death. In fact, they were thrown into a blazing furnace and survived miraculously because of their faith.

One of my favorite startups where I worked early in my career has succeeded beyond all imagination. They are in a rare club known as a Unicorn. They have a valuation over a billion dollars. The founders and early executives committed everything to the startup. In fact, all of us in those early years had dedicated everything. We worked endless hours, spent months on planes and in cars traveling to meetings, wrote millions of lines of code, and did whatever it took to accomplish our goals. The company overcame tremendous growing pains and setbacks through the sheer will to succeed. The challenges would have broken most other startups. I recall several events throughout the time I was there that probably should have caused the company to close their doors. Everyone believed in the vision. The natural result was a team of passionate individuals with unlimited dedication and commitment.

I know many leaders that are, what I call, fair weather leaders. They will work at an organization until things get difficult and then they pick up their chips and move on to the next company. They seldom stick around to experience true dedication in the face of the most difficult of circumstances because they don't want their images tarnished. Their lack of dedication is proportional to their belief.

Dedication forces us to experience the good and

the bad. It is those difficult times that we experience because of our dedication that we become stronger and wiser leaders. The most powerful lessons always come when we face the darkest hour and most difficult situations. Being dedicated means we stick it out. As a result, we learn who we are as a person, a leader, and how we treat others in the face of diversity. I'm grateful for every adverse and difficult situation that I was forced to experience because I am a better person for it.

True success requires us to overcome tremendous obstacles and be entirely committed to our cause. If we as leaders don't believe we can attain our vision then we will never be dedicated to the hard work that is required to accomplish each task. Dedication is dependent upon our belief in our vision.

Questions for reflection:

1. Recall a time when you thought you couldn't possibly continue in a role but somehow managed to persevere.
2. What is it that enabled you to move through the difficult situation?
3. Did your belief in being able to accomplish the goal impact your dedication to the goal?

LESSON 15: COUNSELOR

Galatians 6:2 (GW) Help carry each other's burdens. In this way you will follow Christ's teachings.

The ability to allow a team member to vent without judgment is a secret weapon every leader should learn.

I've spent a great many hours over the course of my career counseling coworkers and team members. I don't ever recall this being in any job description but it definitely comes with the territory. Life and relationships can get messy very quickly. Leaders need to understand this and be in a position to diffuse and refocus our teams.

I learned a very unique tactic many years ago from my wife. There were times that she just needed to talk and vent. She didn't want me to fix the problem, which is my natural tendency. She just wanted to verbalize and talk through a situation to get it off of her chest.

I make a point with my teams that my door is always open to discuss any problem. In fact, I encourage people to come to me, vent, and talk through the problem before they act on it and do something that will cause even more problems for all of us. It's interesting that the act of venting often deescalates the situation so that calmer heads prevail where good and rational decisions can be made.

I find another key skill is being able to listen without condemning and finding fault. Many of the conversations involve personal situations. I could easily take a "more righteous than thou" approach and point out the obvious fallacies in their situations but that shuts down the conversation. I may make suggestions and try to get the person to think about it from a different perspective but again, my role is really to listen.

I don't feel the need to personally solve many of the problems I've been confronted with. I would probably just make things worse in most cases. My objective is for them to always think clearly about the situation and make the best possible decisions on their own. They certainly don't need me to point out their failures. Chances are that they already know that. What they need is someone to hear them out. Simply saying things out loud seems to have a significant impact on how people see their own problems and helps to find a reasonable path forward.

There are many conversations that involve other co-workers, events, and situations that may have come up. In these cases, I will still allow the person to vent and calm down. I will then begin to dig into the facts and if necessary will intervene. I always prefer to have team members work out petty arguments themselves but that doesn't always work out well. I had an employee for some reason think that everyone was always against them. Things escalated and I got a call in the middle of the night while the person was traveling vehemently complaining that the other team members cut off access to voice mail and email. I let the person vent and calm down. As it turned out, the person had accidentally locked the accounts with too many login attempts. They were convinced someone on the team was awake at 3am trying to sabotage them. That person resigned a few weeks later. This was probably a good thing because they were constantly in upheaval and causing problems for the overall morale of the team.

<u>Questions for reflection:</u>
1. Do you permit your team members and co-workers to vent about problems and even personal situations?
2. What techniques do you use to calm the situation and ensure they are on a good path to move forward?
3. How could you improve your current techniques?

LESSON 16: SENSE OF HUMOR

Proverbs 17:22 (NIV) A cheerful heart is good medicine, but a crushed spirit dries up the bones.

Laugh at yourself. It reduces the stress and anxiety that comes with the need to succeed.

I was always very self-conscious as I was growing up. I didn't have much confidence even though I was a talented artist and musician. As a result, when someone called me out for doing something dumb or stupid, I would get offended. I was so naïve. I've since learned to laugh at myself. I still do stupid things and I should probably know better but someone pointing out the obvious doesn't offend me any more.

Highly motivated leaders tend to be single minded and highly focused. Often times, we don't realize how intense we can be. I've often joked with people like this that they need to breathe. I often have to tell myself the same thing. Take a breath, back off, and laugh. Show your team that you are human and that you know how to interact. Laugh at yourself often. If you do something stupid, laugh it off, learn from it, and don't do it again. We all make mistakes. We all have to learn. I know many people that feel that they have to be perfect the first time they try something. Don't put that kind of pressure on yourself. Make the mistakes and laugh.

It is important for leaders to be able to laugh, joke, and create a fun environment for everyone. When I was in college, I worked in the meat department of a local grocery store. The work was hard and oftentimes monotonous. We constantly joked and played practical jokes on each other. One day, someone stuck a wad of nasty meat sawdust in the earpiece of the phone. They paged one of the meat cutters who stuck the phone to his ear and immediately knew he had been pranked. Without missing a beat, he saw the storeowner, and yelled out, "Norm, can you take this call?" Norm proceeded to stick the nasty meat dust in his ear. He shook his head and laughed with us.

Humor can break up the tension of a stressful environment. Having a sense of humor makes us more personable to our team. As with all things, there obviously needs to be a balance. Pranking and joking can quickly escalate from good fun to mean and vindictive acts especially when it comes to political party affiliation and sports teams. We have to be especially careful given the nature of political correctness in our society today.

One of the ways I like to bring humor into the environment is by starting meetings off with a favorite quote and then a cartoon that is relevant to the subject of the meeting. I will especially do this when I know the meeting is going to be confrontational. I want to break the tension and get people to laugh. I find that this opens the door to having a much more productive and less contentious meeting.

There is a really old phrase that I still hear people using today: "Work hard. Play hard." When we create an exciting and fun environment for our teams where they can laugh and be comfortable while being challenged, they will far out perform the teams that are always serious. More importantly, they will bond as a team much more closely which makes them want to stay and produce at a high level. It starts with us. We need to be willing to laugh.

Questions for reflection:
1. Find a way to introduce humor and laughter to your team.
2. What was the result in the team's attitude?

LESSON 17: LOVE AND CARING

1 Corinthians 13:2 (NIV) If I have the gift of prophecy and can fathom all mysteries and all knowledge, and if I have a faith that can move mountains, but do not have love, I am nothing.

***L**ove your team and they will respond in kind.*

I believe a leader must have a loving, caring, and compassionate spirit to be effective. Every person shows this differently but if we don't care for our team, we will never succeed as a leader.

One sales leader I worked with was in the armed services. He was a demanding, sometimes surly, drill sergeant kind of guy. He was quick to let his people know that he was there to get a job done. He demanded results and wouldn't stop until he got what he expected. If someone was missing their number, he was in their face pushing them. Most did not have the chance to see how much he actually cared for the team. If one of his team was hurting or going through a crisis, he had their back. Many would simply give lip service but this leader truly cared.

One of his team members had a child with cancer. My friend went the extra mile. Not only was he able to give excellent advice because of his personal life experience, he made calls and introductions to people that could help the family. His actions showed how he cared.

I have another mentor that runs a small regional software development firm. One of his long-term employees had a terminal illness but was kept on the payroll even after he was no longer able to work. Eventually, the company had to make very tough decisions. It began to struggle to meet payroll and the insurance premiums for everyone skyrocketed because of the individual. In spite of this, the organization still took care of the individual and his family.

I talked about an employee in an earlier lesson that lost his mother the day I was supposed to let him know he was being downsized. A year later when he was working in a different part of the company, he let me know that he'd been in the hospital multiple times and was going to require a liver transplant. We spent a great deal of time on the phone over the next year. He asked me to pray for him and his family on numerous occasions and I was honored to do so. I was heartbroken the day his wife shared with me that he had lost his battle. It felt like I had lost a family member.

For me, the most fulfilling and rewarding side of leadership is caring for those that report to us. There is an obvious expectation that a leader will accomplish the business objectives. The rewards for doing so are typically financial. The benefit for loving and caring for the team are far more rewarding than any financial gains. In fact, there is no comparison. The relationships I've developed with my teams and often their families will last a lifetime. Those relationships are developed over time and by experiencing life together. In every situation, it began by exhibiting love.

Each person has a different love language. We may feel like we are showing that we care by serving or giving gifts but that is not likely everyone's language. Take time to learn what makes each person feel that they are being loved and then act on it when appropriate. You can begin to test this at home with your friends and family. Loving others will benefit all of your relationships.

Questions for reflection:
1. How do you show your team that you care for them?
2. Recall the times that you have gone out of your way to help a person on your team. How did that impact your relationship going forward?

LESSON 18: GENEROUS

Matthew 4:9-11 (NIV) "Which of you, if your son asks for bread, will give him a stone? Or if he asks for a fish, will give him a snake? If you, then, though you are evil, know how to give good gifts to your children, how much more will your Father in heaven give good gifts to those who ask him!

T*he generosity of a leader will be rewarded through loyalty and trust.*

I never gave my kids an allowance. I always felt they needed to earn the money they received. Instead, I tried to give them both quality time and quantity of time. If they had an interest in a particular hobby, sport, or subject, I was all in with them. I went out of my way to ensure their success.

I feel the same way with my team members. I

never give out an allowance or bonus for free but rather, I expect the team to earn it. I'm all in if a team member wants to improve their knowledge, gain experience, advance their career, be mentored, or any other positive action to improve their value. I will find a way to be generous with them based on work schedule, tuition, or whatever it takes. In the end, it benefits the team, the organization, and me.

Similar to our kids, where generosity is most difficult is when it requires both quality time and quantity of time. It's one thing to be generous and allow someone to have flexible hours so they can take care of a family member or attend grad school. It's an entirely different thing to dedicate several hours of my time each week to coach or mentor an employee. Because it requires a personal sacrifice, it is often the most rewarding as well. We are invested in the person and want to see them succeed at whatever they are doing.

I also believe our generosity should span beyond our team and even our organization. There is something special that happens when we volunteer our time, skills, and knowledge to benefit those who can't return the favor. Obviously, those we are helping see value but more importantly, we will grow as a person. This type of generosity takes our focus from being self centered and focused on our own success to making an impact on others.

One of my rock-climbing friends is a schoolteacher in a very underserved urban district. He brings a group of students to the rock climbing gym on a regular basis. I've climbed with some of them and they are talented. He recently took some of the students that were interested to Red River Gorge for a weekend of climbing and camping. These kids come from an environment where that is simply not part of the curriculum. His personal generosity, like most teachers, is highly impacting the lives of his students. He is not the head of a large organization but he is a strong, inspiring, and generous leader, which we could all emulate.

Similarly, I had a favorite schoolteacher in high school that taught history. His tests were extremely difficult. He went the extra mile with his class. He would host study parties after school hours where he would spend as much time as necessary with students to make sure they were ready for the tests. He is now retired but many of us still keep in touch with him and honor his dedication as a teacher.

Questions for reflection:

1. Do you invest generously in the lives of others?
2. Think about the people you invested in. What impact did your investment make in their lives?

LESSON 19: DILIGENCE

Proverbs 21:5 (NIV) The plans of the diligent lead to profit as surely as haste leads to poverty.

D*iligence is only effective when the activity is focused on delivering results.*

Diligence is a mandatory personal attribute. Every successful leader that I know is always focused, planning, contemplating, or physically doing something to move their proverbial ball forward. A primary difference between an average leader and a truly phenomenal leader is focus. The phenomenal leader is diligent on the correct activities all the time, which produces results.

Many executives I know appear to be diligent. They are constantly moving Mach 2 with their hair on fire. There is always a crisis to solve, phones interrupting, people vying for a meeting, and disruption. Managed chaos is not diligence. It's just busy work that fools the person into thinking they are doing great things. Diligence is only effective when the right things are getting accomplished that produce results.

One company I consulted with had a team of business development people who made outbound sales calls to generate leads. In this particular company, the team was paid for the number of calls made. Each person had a specific quota for a number of calls. They were busy making calls all day long. The team was always on the phone talking but no leads where being generated. Week after week, they met their target quotas for calls but there were no results. Unfortunately, when the call details were finally examined, it became evident that the team was simply calling and leaving a voice mail. There was never any active engagement of the customer. They were busy meeting their objective but nothing was getting accomplished. They were obviously being compensated on the wrong metric.

This example highlights the obvious. There are four key areas in which a leader must be diligent to avoid mistakes such as this.

Results: If results aren't produced, the leader will be replaced. It is a simple and timeless principle. For that reason, a leader must be urgently focused at all times on expectations, what progress has been made, how the results are being measured, leading indicators, actual results to date, among others.

Team: The leader must also understand what the team is doing and ensure they are focused on the right things at all times. This doesn't mean micromanaging but it does require having enough understanding to ensure results will be produced and that no surprises are going to derail the forward motion.

Suppliers: Every department or organization is dependent upon others to some degree. A leader must ensure that those suppliers who deliver goods or services are meeting their deadlines. This includes internal departments as well as external organizations.

Risks: A leader must constantly understand and analyze what risks could prevent the team from accomplishing their objectives.

Had the company above focused on these four areas, they would have understood their mistake almost immediately rather than letting it go for months on end.

Questions for reflection:

1. At any given time, can you validate the progress the team is making towards your objectives?
2. Would you be able to justify the value of your team if the executive leadership needed to reduce headcount?

LESSON 20: FAITH

Hebrews 11:1 (NIV) Now faith is confidence in what we hope for and assurance about what we do not see.

T*o have faith is to believe with confidence and certainty.*

There is a saying that has been around for decades. I'm not sure where it originated but it is simple and true. "If you believe you can, then you will." There is a huge chasm between the leader who hopes they will accomplish their goals and one who has faith. Hope tends to be a wish. I hope I win the lottery. I hope this deal closes. I hope I things turn around. Hope is faith without confidence.

Faith on, the other hand, is to believe and have confidence that things will happen because you've seen proof in other areas. There is no guarantee, but you believe emphatically. As an example, we sit in a chair every day. We know the chair will hold us because we've sat in other chairs. We are sure the airplane is going to take off and fly us to our destination because we have flown many times before. We believe that we are going to accomplish our goals because we have done it before and everything is lined up correctly.

There's a story of a young man that strung a cable across Niagara Falls. He yelled out to the crowd gathered around him, "Who believes I can push this wheelbarrow across Niagara Falls?" Most the people in the crowd raised their hands. He jumped up on the cable and carefully walked across the river and back. When he returned he asked, "Who believes I can carry a person across in the wheelbarrow?" Again, all hands were raised. "Who will be the first to go?" At this point, no one raised a hand. They said they believed but their actions proved otherwise.

A leader that has faith will believe with confidence that they will accomplish their objectives. In turn, those around the leader will also believe. Faith is worthless unless it is accompanied by actions. The two work hand-in-hand. I've noticed when my faith is lacking that I can increase it by focusing on my actions. The results of those actions increase my faith. I have a good friend that always says, "I'm gonna fake it 'til I make it." What he means is that he is going to act like he knows what he is doing until he is confident. His actions give him confidence to have faith.

I believe there are different aspects of faith that every leader must have. First, it is critical to believe in one's self. Our teams will see right through us if they know we have doubts. Second, we must trust in our team. If we lack trust, we need to make adjustments, educate, and move people around until we do have confidence.

Finally, we need to have faith in a higher power. What exactly does that mean from a business and leadership perspective? As I discussed in the introduction, many of the difficult decisions we are going to make as leaders force us to reach deep into our belief system. These decisions are going to force us to stand on those principles that have grown out of our beliefs. For me, I'm a Christian. I have faith in God not because I grew up in church but rather because I've seen the evidence of God working in and through me. I know because of my experience, personal relationship, and faith that I can trust those decisions. It is this faith that has molded my deep personal beliefs and gives me the foundation I need to be a leader.

Questions for reflection:

1. How does your faith and belief system impact your decision-making?
2. How does your faith or lack thereof translate to your team?

CHAPTER 3
BEST PRACTICES

The lessons in this final section will highlight best practices of successful leaders. These lessons build upon the fundamentals and personal attributes and show how they are used in practice.

LESSON 21: GRATITUDE OVER CRITICISM

Matthew 7:4 (NIV) How can you say to your brother, 'Let me take the speck out of your eye,' when all the time there is a plank in your own eye?

Give your team reasons to want to work for you. They make a choice daily.

There are many reasons an employee will leave a job. A quick online search shows that a bad and unappreciative boss is always at the top of the list. There's a saying that one doesn't quit a job, they quit a boss. I've certainly found that to be a true statement.

A teacher purposely wrote the first instance of ten equations incorrectly on the board. She could hear the class behind her giggling at the mistake. As she turned around, she said, "I wrote the equation wrong to teach you a lesson. You focused on the one wrong equation rather than all that I got right. The world will never recognize you for all that you do right, it will criticize you for the one wrong thing you did. Rise above the laughter and stay strong."

Many leaders will focus on what's wrong so that they can fix the problem. I find this especially true with men. I know that I am definitely wired this way. The challenge is that our teams may be doing ninety-nine things extraordinarily well but we will zero in on the one thing that needs to be fixed. This communicates loudly that we don't really care about or appreciate the things the team did well. It may come across as bullying, incompetence, harassment or discrimination. It certainly doesn't encourage the team members to want to stay.

I once had a CEO join sales calls and would literally destroy the sales people as they talked about the opportunities. I find that many leaders will zero in on the one negative item in a public setting such as staff meetings. Sales leaders are notorious for this. A sales person may be above plan but the leader calls out the individual because their last deal has gone sideways. What about the other deals that they did close? The sales person gets the impression those closed deals mean nothing and aren't appreciated. In fact, what often happens is that the sales leader has committed to a number and the only way they may be able to attain it is by pressuring sales guys to close opportunities that don't have a chance of closing. The leader is focused on the one negative and not appreciative of all the positive results accomplished.

I have always preferred to use staff meetings to accentuate the positive. I want the team to talk about the things that they have done well so that everyone else on the team can benefit from the ideas and best practices of others. I want to highlight, and show appreciation for the ninety-nine things done well.

I use one-on-one meetings to address problems or correct an individual's actions or poor performance. Even then, I don't typically blame the person and make them feel as though they are failing. Rather, I look for solutions. I will also use the one-on-one meetings to explore the things done well and in most cases ask them to share a particular event or success story on the team call.

When we focus on what the team does correctly rather than calling out their faults, we give them reasons to want to work for us and to excel.

Questions for reflection:
1. Keep a mental count of the times you show sincere gratitude versus correction throughout the day.
2. Does your desire for excellence and focus on the one last issue leave your team feeling unappreciated for the 99 percent done with excellence?

LESSON 22: MENTORING

Proverbs 13:20 (NIV) Walk with the wise and become wise, for a companion of fools suffers harm.

A leader that draws wisdom from trusted mentors and advisors is far more likely to succeed than those that do not.

I've had my share of both good and bad managers over the years. There were many that took me under their wing, taught me, helped me figure things out, and made me a better leader. There were a few that caused me to dread each day not knowing what to expect. I spent time resolving problems they caused rather than accomplishing my own responsibilities.

In one such case, I struggled personally and professionally to be supportive of my manager while not jeopardizing my own integrity and ethics. I constantly reached out to my trusted friends for their advice and counseling to figure out a path forward. It was a difficult time in my life where I had to consider a number of very tough choices. In the end, the board terminated him but not before tremendous damage had been done to the company.

As a leader, you will never have all the answers to each situation. Your strength is in your network of trusted friends, advisors, and counselors. I have the luxury of knowing many extremely talented executives that are always willing to provide feedback and counseling.

I'm fortunate in that I can also turn to my brother who I greatly respect. He runs a technology company and is always more than willing to provide timely advice based on his experiences. I often turn to my wife or parents for advice especially when dealing with people situations. I trust their intuition and ability to see solutions and outcomes that I had not considered.

Often times, we will get contradictory guidance from multiple people regarding how to handle a particular situation. I've been advised to fire a person immediately by one person while another says to give them a second chance. At the end of the day, only we as the manager know the situation first hand and need to determine our path forward. Having multiple points of view is always beneficial and helps us to think through every aspect.

It is equally important to be a mentor to others. Not only does it help the other person but it also strengthens our skills. Consider being a mentor to a person on your team who wants to advance their career or assign one of your team members to be a coach to a less experienced person. We all advanced because someone helped us along the way.

Being a mentor to others on the leadership team is also important even if it is outside of your area of responsibility. Many leadership skills are constant regardless of the area of expertise. Mentoring those in other areas gives us a more holistic understanding of the overall business and increases our own value to the organization.

Another important aspect of mentoring is that trust is developed. The process typically requires that sensitive personal information be shared and by looking for advice, we are making ourselves vulnerable. This builds trust and respect.

Questions for reflection:
1. Identify a list of trusted friends to which you can turn when you need advice or guidance.
2. Identify and engage those on your team that would benefit from being mentored by you or another team member.

LESSON 23: OPEN COMMUNICATION

Philippians 2:3-4 (NIV) Do nothing out of selfish ambition or vain conceit. Rather, in humility value others above yourselves, not looking to your own interests but each of you to the interests of the others.

*O**pen communication requires trust, builds respect, and enables one to look after the interest of others.*

One thing that I constantly see across companies large and small are challenges related to communications. It's easy to understand how communications can become complex in a large company. Surprisingly, I see major challenges in small companies and startups as well.

Open communication is important because it allows the organization to harness the diversity and brainpower of the entire company. Leaders, regardless of how brilliant we think we are, don't know everything. Open communication at the front end of a new endeavor enables the leadership team to get a much broader and deeper perspective from the team. At the backend of the process, it enables the entire organization to be synchronized and pulling in the same direction. Even more importantly, being the recipient of confidential information builds trust and buy-in. The team will respect leaders for trusting them with this information. Some things, such as quarterly results, obviously can't be discussed in an open forum but the concept is the same within those restricted groups.

It makes us feel valuable and that we are making an impact when our ideas are being heard and acted upon. When the team has input into the strategy and direction, they will be more invested and committed to the success of the endeavor.

I find most real conversations happen at the local level through "water cooler" discussions, team meetings, group discussions, and electronic means. I've been in organizations where a key player was terminated and the management team, for whatever reason, chose not to announce the major change. That unnecessarily opened the door for unsubstantiated rumors and speculation.

I'm always surprised about the lack of communication between departments. It seems that many organizations will allow the different teams to gather in their own silo and share minimal information with others. For example, I've seen many occasions where the development team won't share product roadmaps with the sales team because they are concerned the sales team will start telling customers about it rather than selling what is currently available. It's critical that open communication channels be established across all parts of the organization.

Another communication challenge I often encounter is when a leader is an information sinkhole. This person gathers all the data but doesn't trust the team enough to share it. This creates significant problems in that directions are typically mandated versus openly discussed. The team has to trust that the directives coming down from the ivory tower are golden. The team would often be more effective if they had a complete vision of the project or where more connected with the strategy being driven from the top.

Questions for reflection:

1. Do you share highly strategic plans and confidential information with your team?
2. Does the team feel they can provide valuable feedback?
3. Do you make it a practice to solicit feedback from team members and other leaders on a regular basis?

LESSON 24: SETBACKS ARE OPPORTUNITIES

Philippians 1:12-13 (NIV) Now I want you to know, brothers and sisters, that what has happened to me has actually served to advance the gospel. As a result, it has become clear throughout the whole palace guard and to everyone else that I am in chains for Christ.

Challenges, failures, and setbacks are actually opportunities in disguise.

We face challenges every day in our personal and professional lives. Often times, it seems the challenges come in waves and continually beat us down as a shipwreck battered against the rocks. It is critical to approach these challenges with a positive mindset and view them as opportunities.

In the passage, Paul explains that he is in chains because of his mission to share the gospel. I'm fairly confident this was not part of his strategy or business plan. His perspective is interesting; he didn't view his imprisonment as a setback or failure but rather an unintended acceleration of his plan. His message was amplified because of his imprisonment.

Not long after I had joined a new startup, my team told me that our only distributor was going to end our agreement because we were not driving enough revenue. On the surface, this was really bad news. It was a wake up call that enabled us to get in front of the distributor's executive team to discuss the relationship. We created a strategy that benefited both parties and increased revenue for all.

I would like to say that all the technology startups I've engaged were amazing success stories but that is not the reality of entrepreneurship. I had to deal with significant challenges at every company such as product failures, poor leadership, downsizing, inadequate financing, huge egos, bad timing, cultural issues, and even legal issues over intellectual property. It seems that when one challenge hits, others quickly follow. Each of these events shaped me. It may be difficult while going through the crisis but leaders must focus on what can turn the obstacles into positive outcomes that drive optimism across the team.

As a leader, your team members will typically lob

"problem grenades" over the wall for you to fix. I always insist that if someone is going to dump a pile of garbage on my desk that they need to suggest possible resolutions as well. This forces the team to think about it first. More importantly, it empowers them to be part of the solution.

When you face challenges regardless of how big or small, ask yourself the following questions:

- How can we use the challenge to advance our cause in ways we may have never considered?
- What have we learned so that we don't face the challenge again?
- Would the result have been much worse had we not experienced this now?

Questions for reflection:

1. Teach your team to find positive outcomes in every challenge by giving them examples when they come to you.
2. Over time, require that every problem brought to your desk must also include possible ideas for a positive outcome or resolution.

LESSON 25: THE GOLDEN RULE

Matthew 7:12 (NIV) So in everything, do to others what you would have them do to you, for this sums up the Law and the Prophets.

lways treat others with respect, civility, and dignity in the same manner you would expect to be treated.

Civility seems to have been lost in recent years. Society seems to believe that if a group thinks differently, then they must be crushed or defeated. When I first moved into sales, two of the senior sales guys got into an argument over something petty. The disagreement escalated and came to blows. Two grown men wearing suites and ties were on the ground kicking and punching each other. Somehow, it was beyond them to have a reasonable discussion and work out their differences.

"I'm not here to make friends. I'm here to get results." I've heard that statement from many sales VPs and CEOs over the years. This mindset is very prevalent in leadership where success and results are prioritized over the lives of those who create the results. I understand the premise but what a lonely and miserable existence. I've seen the same leaders completely humiliate and destroy the morale of their team members on weekly team or leadership calls all in the name of results. This practice is both shortsighted and self-defeating. It will create a constant turnover of good people. It typically produces results but at a tremendous cost. Turnover is extremely expensive with respect to the cost of hiring, missed opportunity, training, and lost knowledge.

In stark contrast to this mentality is the leader who genuinely cares about their team. Accountability and results can be accomplished while maintaining the dignity of the individual. A sales person who is behind on their number doesn't need to be humiliated in front of the team. They are likely already humiliated by their lack of performance. That conversation is better had in a one-on-one setting where individual coaching can be provided.

My back surgery is another good example. It should have been minor and only caused me to miss about a week of work. The complications I experienced resulted in multiple hospital stays, and a PICC line inserted to deliver antibiotics directly into my heart for the next couple months. The leadership team, coworkers, and team members went above and beyond to ensure my work was covered so that I could take the necessary time to heal. They cared for me and my family, showered us in love, and acted the way I'm sure they would have wanted to be treated. It's a debt that I'll likely never be able to repay.

Successful leaders are able to leverage trusted relationships formed through personal investments and generous application of the Golden Rule. When others are treated in this manner, they will volunteer their assistance and go out of their way to return the favor. Kindness and civility doesn't cost anything but the gains can be infinite.

We should instill this concept into our entire team. Think of how many petty arguments and situations could have been avoided if our team members simply treated each other with respect giving each other the benefit of doubt when there was a question of character.

Questions for reflection:
1. Do you embody the Golden Rule in your interactions with your team? If not, what can you change to make an immediate impact?
2. Does your team treat each other with respect and utilize their differences to make the team stronger?

LESSON 26: SENSELESS WORRY

Matthew 6:24 (NIV) Therefore do not worry about tomorrow, for tomorrow will worry about itself. Each day has enough trouble of its own.

*F**ocus your energy on the things that you can change rather than the things you can't control.*

Some things are easy to say but so difficult to do. This is one of them. There is nothing positive that comes from worrying yet we all do it. If you have kids, you probably worry about them on a regular basis. If you have employees, it is the same. How will you make payroll? How can you entice your employees to stay when you have to double their insurance premiums? We want the best for our teams. When one of them is hurting or struggling with life, we hurt with them and worry for them.

I had a former manager that I highly respect. One of his employees was struggling. He sensed that something was wrong and was worried about her. When he discussed the situation with her, he found out that she was in significant financial trouble resulting from a number of unexpected events. To make matters worse, she had recently purchased a very expensive new car. Instead of worrying about things that he couldn't control, he acted on the things that he could change. He bought the car from her sight unseen and took over her payments. I'm certainly not suggesting that as leaders and managers we should bail our team out of financial difficulties. In this particular case, he had the means, wanted to help, and acted upon it.

I work in the cyber security field. As you might expect, many executives lose sleep because they feel they are sitting ducks waiting for the inevitable phone call that they have been breached. I talked to the CISO (Chief Information Security Officer) of a very large financial institution that was breached a year ago. For months, their brand was tarnished on the evening news and by virtually every trade publication. I expected the CISO to be worried about losing her job, customer perception, lack of adequate security controls, and the many other things out of her control. Her response was insightful. She continued to be focused on areas that she could significantly impact and were she could measurably reduce risk. She had tremendous focus on what could be done to improve customer perception. She clearly understood that there were certain things that she would not be able to control regardless of her actions.

As leaders, we can only impact areas that are in our control. Circumstances are thrown upon us constantly. Recently there have been hurricanes, forest fires, floods, and every other form of natural disaster. It may be within our control to help our employees recover but there is nothing we can do about the events that caused the damage. A large company I was working with made announcements prior to a big hurricane hitting the East Coast for those impacted to take care of themselves. The company would take care of them while they recovered. I know some of them were paid for months before they could actually get back to their day jobs. The leadership was concerned but instead of needless worry, they took action in the areas where they could make an impact.

Questions for reflection:
1. The next time you catch yourself worrying about a situation, make a list of the things that you can and can't control. Prioritize the list and focus on the things that you can impact.

LESSON 27: FAIR AND JUST

Colossians 4:1 (PHILLIPS) Remember, then, you employers, that your responsibility is to be fair and just towards those whom you employ, never forgetting that you yourselves have a heavenly employer.

Life doesn't always treat us fairly, which is all the more reason we should treat others fairly.

Life isn't fair. It never has been and never will be from our perspective. We often question why bad things happen to good people. We all know people who have lost someone to health issues such as cancer, lost a job, been robbed, and so on. It happens and we have no control over it.

As leaders, I can tell you the actions we take are not always going to seem fair to those around us. We make very difficult decisions that have real and oftentimes significant impact on lives. It's rare that you will be able to please everyone. Even what would seem like a simple decision such as assigning a sales quota or a new project could often be considered biased and unfair.

I took over a sales team that was not producing. Significant changes needed to be made. I developed an overall strategy and identified the types of resources I needed. The difficult part was determining who would fill those roles and who would be left out. Could I transition an overlay sales person into a commission based sales person? In this particular situation, I tried everything before I had to make the tough decisions to cut people. Some of those that were cut were talented individuals. They just weren't the people that I needed on the team at that time. I had no place else in the company to place them. The decision making process was logical and as fair as possible. To the people being let go, I'm sure it seemed anything but fair.

When we make a tough decision, we need to be able to support and defend that decision to our leadership team. It's the tough decisions that are going to be questioned, often escalated, and potentially litigated. Our team is also going to question our decisions. We need to be able to show that we acted in the best interest of the organization and the team with utmost fairness.

Where many leaders tend to get into trouble is when they are viewed to have a favorite. It's not uncommon to see leaders have one or two people, I call it the "boy's club", that are treated preferentially. In these situations, a small subset of the team always seems to receive the best projects, assignments, or most profitable opportunities. This creates a tremendous amount of animosity on the team and never ends well. Even if the assignments are based on logical or practical assumptions, other members of the team may still believe it is favoritism. We can't play favorites as leaders but always need to focus on how to best accomplish our objectives and grow our team.

Leaders are never perfect. The decisions we make will never please everyone. Someone will always feel cheated or that they were treated unfairly. Being a leader is difficult. At the end of the day, we must be comfortable with the decisions we have made knowing that we were fair to all and focused on doing the right thing for the organization. Ultimately, every leader needs to realize that we have a higher authority to which we must eventually answer.

Questions for reflection:
1. Can you recall a time when you made a decision that was viewed as unfair?
2. What could you have done to produce a better or more fair result?

LESSON 28: SERVICE ORIENTED

Matthew 23:11-12 (NIV) The greatest among you will be your servant. For those who exalt themselves will be humbled, and those who humble themselves will be exalted.

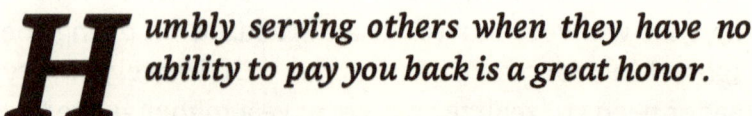

Humbly serving others when they have no ability to pay you back is a great honor.

The United States is a blessed nation. Most people have an overabundance compared to the rest of the world. We are also a very generous nation and give freely of our resources. At the same time, I think we can be prisoners of our success. The more success we have, the more stuff we think we need, and the more time it takes to keep up with it all. When asked to help, most people will simply make a donation because we don't have time to get involved. I'm not suggesting we stop donating to charities but I think we miss the blessing if all we do is send money.

The currency of our lives is time. It's easy to donate money but very difficult to donate time. We can always make more money but we can't add time to our lives. I believe that's why it is so difficult to be truly generous and make a difference.

As a sales person, I've participated in more charity golf events than I care to count. We'll purchase overpriced golf packages for a foursome, buy raffle tickets for stuff we don't need, donate prizes for the raffle, and help the charity raise money. We spend a day on the golf course but we never get our hands messy. Supporting these events are necessary and beneficial but, I feel as a blessed society and leaders that we can do more.

A couple of the Fortune 1000 companies where I have worked encouraged employees to get involved in their local communities through services projects. Some participated in projects as a team building exercise while others participated individually. The result was a tremendous impact on the local communities.

As a leader, I feel it is our responsibility to take the initiative and actually get our hands dirty. We have deadlines and quotas to hit but getting the team together out of the office to focus on others provides long lasting benefits. I think most importantly, it enables us to get our focus off of ourselves and make a lasting impact in the lives of others. Involve the team in the planning so that they are committed and invested. There's nothing worse than someone being forced to serve against their will.

Including a community impact statement in your vision and strategic plan is a good place to start. It ensures you will continue to focus on others. Engage your team and find out what they are passionate about. Encourage the team to involve their families when possible. Then set a time each quarter and get involved in the lives of others.

Get involved with local schools and honor the teachers who get so little respect and appreciation. Deliver gift packages to the teachers who spend their own money to buy supplies for their students. Work with dream centers, homeless shelters, or food pantries. Do yard work for elderly. Visit a nursing home and spend time with the residents. Dress up in costumes and visit a children's hospital. Get out and make a difference in another person's life! I promise you, your team will be the one that benefits the most from the act of service and kindness.

Questions for reflection:
1. Poll your team to learn what they are passionate about.
2. If there isn't one in place, initiate an inaugural community impact day.

LESSON 29: PROFESSIONAL FAMILY

Romans 12:15 (NIV) Rejoice with those who rejoice; mourn with those who mourn. Live in harmony with one another. Do not be proud, but be willing to associate with people of low position. Do not be conceited.

T*hose we work with are our family. Create an environment where everyone lives in harmony.*

Most of us spend nearly half of our waking hours at work. If you are salaried, it is likely even more. These people that we spend so much time with become our second family.

I read an article recently about a company that was struggling. They considered an option to downsize to address the financial shortcoming. They made a tough but calculated decision based on the fact that they valued their team as a family. They asked every employee to take several weeks without pay over the course of a year so that they did not have to let anyone go. An interesting thing happened as a result. People began taking the mandatory furlough time for their coworkers who could not afford to go without a paycheck. They took care of each other. Employee moral and loyalty increased at a time when it should have plummeted. In fact, efficiency increased because everyone worked smarter.

It's important to foster an atmosphere where everyone knows they are part of the family. There are many ways to do this but they all come back to building meaningful relationships. I like to get my team out of the work place to do things together on a regular basis. If it's possible, I love to gather the team at someone's house or restaurant for a meal. It creates a comfortable atmosphere and people don't feel obligated to talk about work. The entire purpose is for the team to develop relationships with each other and even their families.

One of the ways a leader can tell if an employee is going to leave is if they don't have any close relationships on the team. People often stay in a position they don't like because of their friends. If they have no friends, there is less incentive to stay. This is all the more reason to create opportunities for the team to develop relationships.

When you have developed close relationships with coworkers and your team, it gives you the opportunity to live life with them. Celebrate and rejoice with them when they have a big moment such as an engagement, a baby, a new house, or a graduation. These things are important. Be part of each other's lives. Even more importantly, empathize and acknowledge when they live through a difficult or tragic event. Send flowers and a card from the team. Take meals to a family that has suffered the loss of a loved one. I had a manager that came to the funeral of my father-in-law. He gave me tremendous support throughout the process. It makes a difference knowing that your team cares for you and has your back in every situation.

Create a culture that enables your team to live in harmony respecting each other as if they were a close family.

Questions for reflection:

1. Does your team get together outside of work just to hang out?
2. Do you have any team members that don't seem to have any friends in the office?
3. Does your team know and trust each well enough to share personal victories and tragedies?

LESSON 30: ALLOW FOR FAILURE

Luke 22:61-62 (NIV) The Lord turned and looked straight at Peter. Then Peter remembered the word the Lord had spoken to him: "Before the rooster crows today, you will disown me three times." And he went outside and wept bitterly.

*llowing people to fail will enable them to succeed at much greater levels.*

Most people look at failure as a negative. It's not at all. We all have failed. It is how we learn. Most kids don't jump on a bike and start riding immediately. Usually, someone runs along holding the bike up so the fall isn't as bad. Each time they go farther and build confidence. Failure is an important part of the process.

Peter blew it in the passage above. He let Jesus down. It's not long after this that Peter is a completely different person; entirely committed, confident, and on a mission. It's as if he was a caterpillar that went into the cocoon and emerged a butterfly. What changed? He was allowed to fail and he learned from it. It was his failure that enabled success.

If failing is part of the natural learning process, why do we punish people for it in the work environment? I like to encourage people to try things. You don't know if it will work until you try. The key is to manage the risk to ensure that the team is accomplishing the overall objectives. Enabling your team to try and fail gives them confidence to think outside of the box and know they aren't going to be fired for trying to make a difference. Encourage them to fail small and fail quickly. In other words, test the waters. Don't gamble the farm on an idea. Try ideas out on a limited basis before going full scale. As leaders, we have to manage the risk but not stifle the creativity.

During a brain storming session with my sales team, we discussed how to increase lead generation. A member of my team wanted to run a special promotion on a lab system with the idea that it would be a catalyst for purchase of a larger solution. The effort to make this happen was fairly easy. In about a month, everything was ready and the team launched the initiative. We didn't receive a single order based on the promotion. Was this a total failure? I don't think so. We succeeded in knowing this type of promotion would not work for our targeted markets.

There have been many occasions that one of my sales team would come to me with a crazy idea they wanted to try in order to generate interest. One of my team came to me with the idea of hosting a lunch at a nice steak house in Manhattan for senior executives around a particular topic that would be of interest to them. The total cost for the lunch was about $7,500. Most of these events typically attract people with limited decision-making authority who want a free lunch and a few hours out of the office so I was skeptical. In this case, my sales person filled the room with 40 senior VP level prospects that turned into realistic opportunities.

Success is always built on the back of failure so, encourage your team to fail small and fail often. If you think about the sales process, a good sales person may fail a hundred times or more before succeeding to close an opportunity. Failure is not bad, it is part of the natural process of attaining success.

Questions for reflection:
1. Identify one or two failures you have experienced.
2. How did those failures improve your future chances of success?

LESSON 31: ENCOURAGING WORDS

1 Thessalonians 5:11 (NIV) Therefore encourage one another and build each other up, just as in fact you are doing.

simple encouraging word has the power to change lives so give freely.

I traveled all over the US and Canada with a band right out of high school. Rick, the oldest member, had the most natural ability to encourage others that I have ever seen. He didn't use fake, insincere flattery. Instead, his encouragement came from the heart and was genuine even with people whom we had just recently met.

Encouragement is not something that comes naturally for me. It's a skill that I continually practice and force myself to improve. I've come to realize that it is also one of the most powerful tools we have as humans to make a positive impact on those around us. We often have no idea of the challenges that those around us are experiencing. Offering sincere and heartfelt encouragement could be the ray of sunshine they need to get them through the day.

Not only does a sincere word of encouragement have the magical ability to impact someone's entire day for the better, it lets the person know that you are paying attention to that specific behavior or activity and that you specifically noticed them. I will often encourage team members in front of others when they do something that everyone should be doing. It draws attention to the good behavior rather than trying to punish the bad behavior.

I want to provide a word of caution about too much encouragement. The goal isn't to hand out flattery like participation awards but rather to highlight and acknowledge behavior that you want replicated. I view comments on superficial things like clothes, hair, and shoes to be participation awards. Focus on the behavior. "I appreciate the help you provided on the proposal without being asked. You saw a need and addressed it." "The way you handled the conflict in our meeting with Operations was exemplary. You made your points calmly and succinctly even when they started yelling. I was proud of you."

Another unique attribute of encouragement is

that it doesn't cost us anything yet it is often priceless. I don't know of many best practices that deliver such a high rate of return. If, like me, this is an area you struggle then let me make a few suggestions to get started. Start by making a list of behaviors you feel need to be improved. Highlight the type of behavior you want modeled at your staff meetings and then watch specifically for the team members that display the correct behavior. Highlight those positive behaviors during the next staff meeting. Continue to do this over several weeks and your team will understand that this is important to you.

Change your negative tone during meetings to positive affirmations. Pay attention to the actions that deserve recognition and call them out. "Gary, your code passed all the testing gates on the first pass. Great job." "Cindy, your forecast of committed deals was 96% accurate and has been linear throughout the quarter. That really helps the development team forecast what to build. Great job!" This is going to take some practice if you are not a natural encourager. Start by practicing at home and with your friends. They may think your crazy at first if it is out of character but the rewards will be worth it.

Questions for reflection:
1. Is your tone with your team generally encouraging?
2. Are you more focused on gaps or accomplishments?

LESSON 32: SHARPENING IRON

Proverbs 27:17 (NIV) As iron sharpens iron, so one person sharpens another.

***I**n order to solve the challenges of tomorrow, we must improve our knowledge and skills today.*

I worked in a meat department all through high school and college. We used a tool called a honing steel to sharpen our knives. Most home cutlery sets come with one and it is never used. It's a simple tool. The blade is run across the steel to sharpen the edge hence the phrase, steel sharpens steel.

I always chuckle to myself when young adults in high school or college tell me they are tired of studying, learning, and taking tests. The reality is that school simply prepares us for a lifetime of learning. In fact, I probably read and study more consistently today than

I ever did in college. It is the only way to stay relevant.

Millennials are growing in numbers in the workforce. They have a very different view of life compared to those of my generation. It's both refreshing and challenging at the same time. As leaders, we must be able to adapt. The tried and true tools and techniques that we used to manage in the 80's simply won't work with this generation. I was speaking with a friend that told me he was tired of babysitting his Millennial employees. I suspect his young team is equally tired of his inability to meet their needs. Their generation doesn't respond like others. The next generation will be different as well. That is not a bad thing. Leaders need to continuously adapt and learn new ways to inspire. The only constant we have is ongoing change.

I observed an experienced (and by that I mean older) sales leader hire a group of college interns to focus on sales development. He tried to incentivize them the same way he did his sales teams in the past. It was a total failure. These young adults didn't care about working endless hours in order to make a huge commission check. Their motivation was entirely different. The sales leader needed to sharpen his tools. In fact, in some cases, he needed new tools. As leaders, we must constantly be refreshing and replacing our tools.

It is equally important for us as leaders to continually sharpen the skills of our team. One CEO I have worked with described how he does this. He always pairs new and typically younger college graduates with a very senior person as a mentor. I expected him to say his reasoning was to teach the younger person but that was not the case. It obviously provided structure and experience to the younger people but something much more exciting happened. He noticed that the senior people would tend to get stuck in a rut of doing things the same way. By pairing them with younger people, it sharpened the skills and imagination of the senior people.

As a leader, we must constantly challenge, encourage, recognize, and reward our teams for improving their skills and knowledge. Likewise, we must also continually focus on improving our own skills and abilities. The speed of change in our society has accelerated beyond anything we have ever experienced. If we are going to be relevant and address the problems we face in the future, we need to start preparing today. If we simply stand still and rest, we are losing ground.

Questions for reflection:

1. Identify practices or skills that have become dated or don't seem to be as productive as they once were.
2. Implement a training plan that will modify or improve the skills and techniques.

LESSON 33: MINDSET OF THE TEAM

Philippians 4:13 (NIV) I can do all this through him who gives me strength.

team *can only succeed when it believes it can succeed.*

This has always been one of my favorite verses. To add some context to this, Paul was in chains for sharing the gospel when he wrote these words. What I find most interesting is that in spite of his circumstances, Paul is encouraging those that are concerned about him.

One of the things my dad always said to me as I was growing up is, "You can do anything if you just put your mind to it." That is a philosophy and mindset I have always lived by similar to the verse above. As I've grown older, I realize that even though I believe my team can do all things, what is most important is if we should do them at all? What value is there in attaining this goal or event that we have set out to accomplish? If it is a large and audacious goal, it will likely take significant effort and commitment. Is it worth the valuable time and efforts of my team?

These are the same questions every single person on your team will wrestle with over time. In fact, you will need to overcome many doubts in your team. Why am I killing myself for this? Can we really do this? Is the sacrifice I'm making for this team worth it? Do I believe in this vision?

I believe it is the leader's job to instill this mindset into our teams. This is why vision, passion, strategy, and focus are so important. Our vision gives us direction. It is WHAT we are going to accomplish. Passion is the reason or WHY we will succeed. It is the driver that compels us to push forward against all odds. Strategy is the plan that shows HOW to get there. And focus impacts WHEN we will get there. I firmly believe we can accomplish anything when these four ingredients come together.

It is each of these fundamental activities that answers the questions that your team will pose throughout the process. I was watching a YouTube channel last night about a group of guys that started a company called Yes Theory. They have a concept that there is no such thing as a stranger. They produce video content of crazy things they have done such as getting complete strangers to go skydiving on the spur of the moment or sending total strangers on a blind date to another country. As they were growing their company, they encountered every one of these questions and doubts. It was their ultimate belief and mindset that resulted from their vision, passion, strategy, and focus that have enabled them to carry on. Why are people following them? I think it's quite simple. Their followers are entertained initially but soon realize that the message moves and impacts them in a very special way.

Our ability to instill our mindset and belief into our team is paramount to our success as a leader. It starts with believing in ones self. Only when we truly believe that we can accomplish our goal will we be able to make others believe.

Questions for reflection:
1. Review your vision and strategy.
2. Do you believe in it passionately to the point you live, breath, and dream about it?
3. Is it worth your time to do what is necessary to succeed?

LESSON 34: BALANCE VERSUS HARMONY

Ecclesiastes 3:1 (NIV) There is a time for everything, and a season for every activity under the heavens:

We were created to live life to the fullest. Why do we compromise?

I was given a very special gift. I don't believe I was at the point of death but I was headed in that direction quickly. My recovery from bacterial meningitis was an awakening - a new lease on life. It put all of my priorities into perspective.

I have not conducted an interview since that day where I don't talk about the importance of prioritizing one's life. I tell the potential employees that I expect them to be at their kid's soccer game, their daughter's wedding, and at their partner's side through major life events. Those are moments that we never get back. I've never heard anyone laying on their deathbed say, "I just wish I worked a few more hours and gained that promotion."

I prioritize my life into four primary buckets in the following order: Faith, family (and friends), self, and career. Consistent and constant investments are required for the buckets to remain full and balanced. When we try to balance our lives, it implies that we take away from one area in order to invest in another. For example, if I focus on my career, then I take away from family. I prefer to look at these four buckets as being tightly integrated because they are. Investments that I make into my family, self, and faith should show results in my career. If one bucket is empty, the remaining buckets are eventually going to suffer as well. Each part of our lives works in harmony with the others. That's why I find it important for each person on the team to ensure they are investing into every bucket. An employee that is happily invested in their family is going to be someone that is more pleasant and confident at work and vice versa.

I know plenty of people who invested everything into their careers ignoring family, their own health, and certainly faith only to find themselves lonely and miserable having lost what really mattered to them. They have no faith to ground them when major life events happen. You might think the person that is 100 percent invested in their career is the ideal person to have on the team. I don't think so. That person may be a high performer for a while but they are typically high maintenance as well. They are going to bring baggage to work in the form of divorce, problems with kids, health issues, and so on.

Living life to the fullest requires us to live a life of harmony. It necessitates that we prioritize and make room for the different things that are important for each particular season of your life. We need to continually adjust over time as our circumstances and needs change. For example, we will invest in the four buckets very differently when we are just starting out our career compared to the person who has young kids, or someone who has gone through a life-changing event.

You should embrace your team as they seek this difficult and ever-changing balance. They are going to come into the office energized by their family. Their faith is going to carry them through the challenges that we all experience. They are going to energize their family because of their work. If a team member needs flexible hours to take care of an aging parent or sick child, find a way to make it happen. We live in a world of mobility. Your team is going to reap the rewards.

Questions for reflection:

1. Identify and prioritize the 3 most important things to you in each of the buckets: Faith, family, self, career.

LESSON 35: BEHAVIOR PROBLEMS

Matthew 18:15 (NIV) "If your brother or sister sins, go and point out their fault, just between the two of you. If they listen to you, you have won them over."

Failure to correct bad behavior leads to failure as a leader.

A leader must take corrective action when necessary to benefit the team. I know people who love confrontation. They have no problem getting in another person's face and telling them how they feel. That has never been my style. There are an infinite number of ways to adjust behavior but fortunately, there are some common traits.

I've never liked 360 reviews but it is one method of getting feedback and correcting. I've never been a fan of these because correction needs to be accomplished very close to the event. I once had a manager who I highly respected and trusted. I learned more about leadership from him than anyone since. One thing he needed to work on was how he confronted people. I'd seen him yell at people over something they did in front of the rest of the team. I felt it was inappropriate. Later that year, the CEO asked me to complete a 360-degree review and to provide three things that were positive and three that needed work. I highlighted this situation and framed it in a positive light. A short time later, I got a call from my manager who was furious about his review. The CEO took my words out of context and named me. Our relationship was never the same after that. He felt that I had betrayed him, which couldn't have been further from the truth.

This highlights a number of important points that I want to make. When you are correcting someone, go to the person first. Don't write or say things to other people because that could leak or deteriorate into gossip. If you talk behind someone's back or write emails, it will get back to them. This brings up a critical point. Don't say or write anything that you are not willing to say directly to the person. I strongly recommend you talk to the person. They may not even realize what they are doing is a problem. Have the courtesy and respect to speak to the person privately and discuss the issue. Usually, this will be the end of it. Often times, the person with the poor behavior may not report to you but their actions impact your team's performance. Talk to the person privately first and inform them the action needs to change. If they don't change, then escalate it to their manager.

Deal with the poor behavior immediately rather than waiting for an upcoming review. Don't ignore it with the hope that it will get better. Hope is not a good business strategy. It won't improve unless you address it. If the behavior continues, you will need to escalate your actions. Consult with your human resources team if necessary especially in the case of violence, aggression or harassment of any kind. Regardless, do not let it fester.

The rest of the team is watching to see how you handle the behavior. If you ignore the behavior or overreact, you will lose the respect of the team. Get the facts so that you can address the situation privately, quickly, and fairly. If others are impacted, speak to them but the details don't need to be shared. There have been occasions where I will also address the expectations related to behavior in a larger more public forum such as a staff meeting if warranted but I will never call out individuals.

Questions for reflection:

1. Identify occasions where behavior issues were not addressed quickly. What will you do differently next time?

LESSON 36: LACK OF PERFORMANCE

Matthew 25:24-25 (NIV) "Then the man who had received one bag of gold came. 'Master,' he said, 'I knew that you are a hard man, harvesting where you have not sown and gathering where you have not scattered seed. So I was afraid and went out and hid your gold in the ground. See, here is what belongs to you.'

Lack of performance is contagious and must be addressed.

The passage above is a small section from the "Parable of the talents". Three servants are each given an amount of gold to invest while their master is away. The first two double what they were given and the third servant hid the gold. We discussed behavioral problems in the last lesson. This lesson is focused entirely on performance.

Sometimes, we take a chance on a person and it simply doesn't work out. Other times, a person who typically performs well gradually begins to slide into a level that is not acceptable. Unfortunately, leaders are in our position to produce results and can't typically carry a person that is not performing. We don't get participation awards for showing up. Leaders get recognized, promoted, or fired because of the results of their teams. If we let one person slide with mediocre effort, the rest of the team will quickly follow. Why would they work harder if there were no consequence for not performing?

Leaders need to identify early that one of our team members is slipping or not performing. The earlier we can address the performance problem, the more likely we can produce a positive outcome. Our primary concern should be to resolve the performance problem rather than get rid of the person.

My first discussion with the team member is usually direct and factual. My goal is to make the person aware that they are not meeting expectations and to understand what might be causing the problem. I'll ask the person to develop a plan of action to get back on track. I'm looking for specific activity, metrics, and dates based on my expectations.

Upon receiving the "get well plan", I begin tracking the progress, discussing activity and results in more detail at our regular meetings, and formally documenting discussions. This certainly lets the person know that past performance isn't satisfactory and ideally, the increased focus gets the person back on track. Replacing an individual should be the last resort because of the impact to the business and the employee's life. It means admitting to some degree that we have failed as a leader. It takes our focus off of our main objective of producing results.

We often get caught up in the emotion of letting a person go but we must step back and look at the big picture. Our failure to act on one person could result in the entire team being eliminated because of poor performance. When I feel I must let a person go, I don't disparage or throw them under the bus in front of the team or even in person. I don't tell everyone that they weren't performing. I try to let them go with dignity and respect and expect the same treatment in return. In the end, the team will understand your course of action and highly respect your decision. Regardless of the reaction, you must make the decision that you feel best serves the organization.

Questions for reflection:

1. Do you measure your team against expectations regularly in order to avoid performance problems?

LESSON 37: HIRING THE RIGHT TEAM

Proverbs 26:10 (NIV) Like an archer who wounds at random is one who hires a fool or any passer-by.

A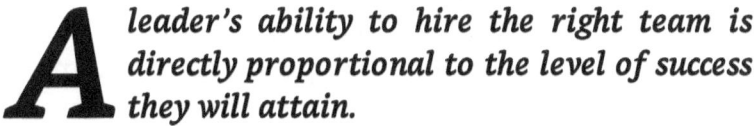 leader's ability to hire the right team is directly proportional to the level of success they will attain.

On the surface, this principle seems obvious. In practice, it is an extremely difficult challenge. Many leaders have failed or experienced major setbacks because of bad hires. Chances are if you have hired more than a few people, at least one of those hires didn't turn out as you expected. They goal is to limit the bad hires.

The first and most important aspect of hiring the

right person is to define what you need. Strategy always comes before organizational structure. In other words, figure out how many people you need, where they need to be located, what they will do, how much they can do, how they will be managed, and when you need them.

I'm not going to go in to details on all the steps of hiring. There are plenty of materials and articles to help you through the process of posting your positions and interviewing. You will typically have an internal HR department or recruiter to assist you. I want to focus on the characteristics of the person that will give you the "right" team. I've prioritized the qualities that I look for when hiring.

Character: Can I trust the person to represent my brand? Do they have integrity? Spend some time on this to ensure you are getting what you think. Compare their resume to their LinkedIn profile. Look at their social media. Ask their references and more importantly, mutual friends. Ask detailed questions in the interview process about things they've written in their resume. You can't change a person's character.

Organizational fit: The greatest person in the world on paper may be a terrible decision for your team. Ensure the potential candidate will compliment the culture, add diversity, and value.

Passion: I like to hire people that are full of energy and excitement. They tend to be "hungry" and have "fire in their belly". These are the people that understand urgency and will get things done. At times, they are harder to manage because you may need to hold them back or keep them on focus. I would rather deal with that any day over trying to motivate a person to move.

Ability: Does the person have the knowledge, physical stamina, aptitude, and skills to accomplish the job? This is typically the easiest characteristic to validate.

Relevant experience: Have they done a similar role before? Can they translate similar experience into success in this role?

Desire to grow: Do they have ambitions to improve their skills and move to the next level of success? Could they potentially be a replacement for me when I am promoted? This concept scares many leaders because they feel they need to be the smartest one on the team. I like to hire smart people because they make me look smarter.

History of success: Can they show they have a history of success related to the role? I like to focus on two types of success: Actions that lead to results and obstacles that were overcome.

When these characteristics are met, chances are that you will have a great employee. You will need to be creative to validate the characteristics but it is worth it.

Questions for reflection:
1. Define your prioritized list of qualities for hiring.
2. How can you tell if the person has these qualities?

LESSON 38: MATURING LEADERS

James 1:2-4 (NIV) Consider it pure joy, my brothers and sisters, whenever you face trials of many kinds, because you know that the testing of your faith produces perseverance. Let perseverance finish its work so that you may be mature and complete, not lacking anything.

It is the testing of our leadership skills that make us highly effective and wise leaders.

Let's face it. We are going to face an abundance of challenges and trials throughout our career as a leader. Most of us dread those challenges. The reality is that we should look at the trials as a test to ensure that we are maturing and succeeding as a leader. This sounds counterintuitive. Who in their right mind wants to experience problems? The reality is that those challenges help us to persevere and mature.

I firmly believe that if you want ensure you know material you have been studying, teach it to someone else. If you want to ensure that the knowledge will hold up in the field, put it to the test.

When I first started rock climbing in a gym, I could not fathom lead climbing the overhung routes. When my skills progressed to the point I could technically make the moves, I realized that I had a perseverance problem. I forced myself to climb laps on less challenging routes. It was difficult but gave me the endurance and perseverance needed to climb the harder routes.

We need to look at trials and tests as a way to improve our skills and endurance. The first time we experience a problem, we might be overwhelmed and somewhat tentative in our response. The more we see similar problems, the more quickly and confidently we will be at handling it. Eventually, we reach the point that we anticipate a problem and prepare for it so that it never happens at all. That is maturity.

I was still a new climber the first time I climbed outdoors at Red River Gorge in Kentucky. I felt pretty confident in the gym but I can clearly remember lying against the slab barley able to hang on. I was thinking, "I must be insane." I was five feet above my last draw and five feet away from the next. I was paralyzed and couldn't move. Gravity helped out and I took my first big "whipper" on real rock and fell about 15 feet landing softly as the rope caught. I realized very quickly that even though outdoor climbing was different, there were a lot of things that were the same. It was much less frightening after that experience.

It's the same with leadership. We are often going to be forced into situations and circumstances we have never faced before. If we simply look back to all the trials and testing that we've gone through we will realize that this challenge is not so different. We won't be paralyzed or afraid to make a decision. We will overcome and excel because of the challenge.

Challenges, trials, and tests are our friends. They are the very tools needed for us to grow. It's through these events that we develop our leadership muscle and perseverance. Embrace each trial and know that you will be a better leader when you work your way through it.

Questions for reflection:
1. Begin keeping a journal of major challenges.
2. Are there similarities to those you faced before?
3. Have your skills in resolving the challenges improved by knowing what you did the last time?

LESSON 39: POSITIVE CULTURE

Matthew 13:8 (NIV) Still other seed fell on good soil, where it produced a crop – a hundred, sixty or thirty times what was sown.

*positive culture breeds a positive team and extraordinary results.*

The verse above is from the "Parable of the sower". It's a story is about a farmer who planted seed. Some of the seed fell in areas that weren't conducive to growth. The only seed that grew well was the seed that was planted in the good soil. The culture we create as leaders is like the soil in which we plant a garden. Our teams are only going to excel and produce results a hundred fold when we create an atmosphere conducive to growth.

Two of my top criteria when I am considering a

company for employment are the leadership team and the culture they have created for their employees. The culture is sometimes difficult to see from the outside. It is always insightful to compare the executive's view of company culture with that of the line staff and on-line reviews.

What are the characteristics of a company with a positive culture where employees thrive?

- Clearly articulated vision, mission, and purpose
- Passionately focused
- Honest and open communications
- Code of conduct: Integrity, trust, and respect
- Invest in people, diversity, and recognition
- Fun, exciting, impactful, and personally fulfilling
- Committed to excellence

Culture must be implemented from the top down. The leadership team must embrace, embody, and enforce the corporate culture on a daily basis. It must be part of the daily conversation from the CEO and board to the person at the bottom of the org chart. If the culture and corporate ethics and values are important to the leaders, it will be important to everyone.

It is each leader's responsibility to develop a positive culture for our area of responsibility that folds in the corporate values. If we want to improve productivity then invest in the team and improve the culture. A strong and positive culture always impacts productivity.

I've been at a couple companies that were forced to downsize or file for bankruptcy protection. The culture is almost always negatively impacted. Fun and excitement are replaced by fear and worry. Productivity grinds to a halt. Those that were not cut in the layoffs begin to jump ship. Everyone begins to move to a mode of self-preservation rather than being concerned about the values of the company.

I've also been at startups that weathered major storms because of their culture. One in particular had a record year of sales only to find out that a majority of the product shipped had a faulty component. Based on the company's culture and values, the leadership team made the investment to replace every faulty product. In spite of that setback, we continued to make an impact and had fun doing it. I am still good friends with everyone I worked with there. That is the power of a strong culture. It builds trust and relationships that can overcome any hurdle.

Questions for reflection:
1. How do you embody the corporate values within your team?
2. Do you recognize and reward those that stand above the others in how they embody the core values defined in the culture?

LESSON 40: DIVERSITY

1 Corinthians 12: 17, 20, 26 (NIV) If the whole body were an eye, where would the sense of hearing be? If the whole body were an ear, where would the sense of smell be? ... As it is, there are many parts, but one body... If one part suffers, every part suffers with it; if one part is honored, every part rejoices with it.

Augment your personal weaknesses by hiring people that act and think differently from you.

There are many reasons to have people of diverse backgrounds and thinking on your team. The most important aspects to me are the increased depth, creativity, and expanded capability. If everyone I hired had the same skills and viewed the world exactly the same as me, the team would be very one-dimensional. Like the passage above, the team would be like a big eyeball with no other capabilities.

There are obviously certain skills and characteristics that need to be met when building a team. For example, if I'm building a software development team, the people need to be able to write code. Even though the code may be structured, the diversity brings unique capabilities into problem solving and creativity. For example, a teacher, an artist, and a sales guy who have turned to software development will approach a concept much differently than the guy who has been programming 40 years. Each will bring their unique vision and experience to the functionality of the solution.

We all have strengths and weaknesses as an individual and as a team. It's critical that we build our team with people that augment the overall team. For example, I typically manage sales teams. Some people have an uncanny ability to make cold calls all day long while most people hate that aspect of sales. Others are good at selling direct. Still others sell indirect through channels and resellers. Some are good at documentation and process while others are a bull in a china shop. I want all of these personalities on my team because they teach each other and augment each other's skills.

I've talked mostly about diversity of capabilities to this point. Diversity in demographics, cognition, and experience such as culture, thinking, race, gender, age, and whatever other classification are also critical.

As I've mentioned repeatedly, there is more to work than accomplishing a task and collecting a paycheck. As people, we all need to stretch our minds and learn to appreciate others in our professional and personal lives.

Professionally, I've had the privilege of working with just about every diversity classification imaginable. I love it because it enables me to appreciate different viewpoints and see through the eyes of others. I'm a better person for it. We become a more enlightened and caring team once we move past tolerance to love, respect, and appreciation of differences.

To me, the most important aspect about diversity is that it enables much more creativity and depth when I tap into those unique attributes of each person. It does no good to hire a person that thinks differently than me and force them to fit my mold. The fact that they think differently is an asset that should be respected and applied.

Questions for reflection:
1. Write out a list of your strengths and weaknesses.
2. How do the people on your team magnify your strengths and augment your weaknesses?

LESSON 41: DELEGATION

Genesis 41:41-42 (NIV) So Pharaoh said to Joseph, "I hereby put you in charge of the whole land of Egypt." Then Pharaoh took his signet ring from his finger and put it on Joseph's finger. He dressed him in robes of fine linen and put a gold chain around his neck.

L*eaders must delegate both tasks and authority in order for the team to succeed.*

Delegation has always been difficult for me when I know I can do the task more efficiently and accurately. It drives me crazy when I assign a task to someone and they need to ask me a ton of questions. I could have completed the task on my own more quickly. I am also a perfectionist so I struggle when someone whom I've delegated a task completes the work differently or with less care than I would like. I suspect I'm not the only leader that struggles with these issues.

There are many reasons that leaders must delegate. First of all, we simply can't do it all on our own. If we could, we wouldn't need a team. We hire a team to split up the workload. The second reason is that it gives our team members the opportunity to grow, learn, and be stretched out of their comfort zone. Another benefit of delegation is that it builds trust and respect.

The key to delegation is to define the expectations. What is it you need accomplished? When does it need to be completed? What does success look like? What are the milestones? What authority does the person have in completing the task? Once the expectations are set, you need to walk away and trust the person to get the job done. Check in on the progress on a regular basis and offer guidance as necessary. The key is trust. Trust them to figure out how to get it done. We hire good people so we need to let them do the job we hired them to do.

I had an employee that worked with resellers on a regular basis but they had never built a channel sales strategy. Creating a strategy is a much different task than implementing one. We both struggled through the process often butting heads out of frustration. I had created and implemented many channel strategies over the years and had in mind the specific tasks needed. The person came at it from an entirely different perspective and view. The end result is not what I would have done but they needed to own it and manage it so it ultimately worked out. My goal was not to tell the person how to do it but let them learn and become a much more valuable to me in the long run.

I tend not to delegate a task to someone that already knows how to do it. For them it becomes busy work stacked on top of everything else that needs to get done. I typically assign the task to someone who hasn't done it and point to the more experienced person as a resource. I know it is going to take longer and may not be at a level that I would like. I take that into account when assigning the task. I do this so that I build capability on the team. If my more experienced person leaves, I need someone that can step in. More importantly, delegating in this manner grows the entire team making every person more valuable when they are stretched beyond their level of comfort.

Questions for reflection:

1. Create a list of tasks or projects that you could delegate that would help a team member gain important leadership experience.
2. What do you do to ensure the tasks and projects you assign get done to your expectations?
3. What things could you do that will improve outcomes?

LESSON 42: PERFECTION OR RESULTS

Philippians 3:12-14 (NIV) Not that I have already obtained all this, or have already arrived at my goal, but I press on to take hold of that for which Christ Jesus took hold of me. Brothers and sisters, I do not consider myself yet to have taken hold of it. But one thing I do: Forgetting what is behind and straining toward what is ahead, I press on toward the goal to win the prize for which God has called me heavenward in Christ Jesus.

***P**erfectionism is an unrealistic expectation that severely impacts real results.*

There is a fine balance between perfection and achieving results. The challenge with perfection is that it is very difficult to attain. There is a point of diminishing returns when the amount of time and effort that is required to reach perfection ceases to be worth the return. It is the leader's job to find the appropriate balance.

There was a joke I heard when I was studying to become an engineer. A mathematician and an engineer are competing to get to a beautiful lady. They are only permitted to move half the distance of their previous move. The mathematician didn't bother to move knowing mathematically, he could never reach her. The engineer started running because he knew from a practical perspective, he could get close enough. I have to regularly fight the temptation to be a perfectionist as a leader. I've learned that "close enough" is usually sufficient for my needs to drive results. I also struggle to not force my need for perfection on others.

Life and leadership is a journey that each of us is on. We will never be at a point in life where we can claim perfection. We continue to press on towards our goal to be perfect but like the engineer in the story, we need to accept that "close enough" is usually more than sufficient.

It is critical for a leader to be able to distinguish between the pursuit of perfection and the need to accomplish real results. I was working with a marketing team to develop a technical sales presentation. The key person on the project took the draft that I had developed and added the necessary content I requested. He also made major changes to the formatting, messaging, design, and overall look. A month later, he was still debating certain wording and visuals. While he continually drug the project out, I took what I thought was the "good enough" version and began using it with customers. The specific items that he was spending such an inordinate amount of time on went completely unnoticed by every customer. I had to produce results. I couldn't afford perfection.

Every leader obviously wants to turn out the most professional and perfect product possible but at some point they will realize they're at a point of diminishing returns and move forward. Every program manager responsible for software development has a bug list and feature roadmap. If he waited for the code to be perfect, it would never be released at all. All leaders strive to produce the best product as possible with the given resources. We must never forget that the ultimate goal is to produce results.

Questions for reflection:
1. Are you a perfectionist?
2. Do you drive your team nuts demanding their work reach unrealistic perfection?
3. What can you do to become comfortable with "good enough"?

LESSON 43: MOLEHILLS OR MOUNTAINS

Ephesians 4:26-27 (NIV) "In your anger do not sin": Do not let the sun go down while you are still angry, and do not give the devil a foothold.

*ddress problems as molehills before they become a mountain range.*

I suspect most of us have ignored a problem thinking it was insignificant and would go away only to find out that when it resurfaced, it had grown exponentially. I especially find this true with behavior problems.

Early in my career, I had two technicians on my team that didn't get along. They were always picking on each other and for some reason could not work together. One thing that annoys me is when people on the same team can't figure out how to get along. I knew they were bickering and assumed they could work out their differences as adults. Things escalated between them. They were hiding each other's equipment, undermining each other at every turn, and becoming verbally abusive. Eventually, I had to call them in my office and have a "come to Jesus" discussion. I ended up moving them both to different facilities but not until after they had irreparably damaged any relationship they might have had with each other. I should have acted much sooner.

The majority of my executive management has been focused on channel sales where I used resellers to represent and sell our solution. One of the frequent challenges I continually faced early on was that a reseller would introduce our product to a customer and then one of my company's sales people would cut the reseller out of the opportunity. Needless to say, these became extremely large "mountains" very quickly. I learned to avoid these explosive situations by establishing rules of engagement and training the sales people. It enabled me to circumvent the problem when it was small prior to blowing up. Circumstances would still happen occasionally where a customer insisted on going around the reseller but it was a controlled conversation that could be managed.

There are many types of situations that can quickly expand from a molehill to a mountain. At one early stage startup, we had extended a line of credit to our resellers. One of the more active resellers had a number of customers closed and owed us over a million dollars. They started missing payment deadlines on multiple orders but our finance team didn't freeze their credit because they were delivering extremely large and profitable deals. Unfortunately, that company filed for bankruptcy. We were paid pennies on the dollar as part of the settlement. The situation could have been avoided early on by freezing the credit and forcing them to get their financing externally. That mistake cost our company dearly and should have been addressed when it was a small problem.

I also firmly believe in this principle from a personal perspective. My wife and I don't argue too often but when we do, we make certain that we don't go to bed angry. We may not agree but we are on the same team. Letting days go by without coming to a resolution or understanding is bad for any relationship. What was once a small disagreement can quickly escalate into an all out battle. It is always better to resolve an issue when it is small.

Questions for reflection:
1. Recall a situation that recently escalated or exploded.
2. Where there early warning signs that there may have been a problem looming?
3. What can you do in the future to prevent something similar?

WRAPPING THINGS UP

Each significant action a leader takes is influenced, driven, or impacted because of an emotion tied to the love / hate spectrum. The depth of that emotion is visible in the intensity of our action. In addition, these emotions may be directed inwardly or externally. As corny as this sounds, love for others is the basis and an underlying theme throughout this book. As I said in the introduction, much of leadership requires us to understand and trust in our core values. For me, those values are based on faith and deeply permeated with love for others. Many leaders have succeeded with a foundation based on a love for self or even hate for others but those are typically not the people I want to work for or with.

Success is usually thought of in terms of financial gain. Most companies hire leaders to ultimately drive financial gain. I was recently reminded of a concept that I've heard over the years. If, at the end of our lives, all we have is a huge bank account, then we have failed miserably. Success is not measured in money but in moments, relationships, and how deeply we impacted others. My desire for you as you reflect on these leadership lessons is that you are not only the best leader you can be but that you succeed in all areas of your life: career, family, relationships, self, and faith. Review these concepts regularly and embed them into your daily routine. More importantly, share them with others. As I discussed these concepts with friends in the business community, I repeatedly had people tell me they thought I was talking about their boss when hearing the examples of failures and what not to do. There are plenty of bad leaders that could improve if we all do our part to enable the principled leaders of today and tomorrow to have integrity, vision, and care about others.

ABOUT THE AUTHOR

CHUCK PLEDGER is an accomplished business executive, consultant, author, and blogger focusing primarily on topics relating to entrepreneurship, sales acceleration, cyber security, relationships, and management consulting. Much of his 30 plus year career has been at the senior executive level of technology startups. **His passion and life mission is to inspire and positively impact the lives of those around him.**

When not focused on career, he loves spending time with his family, rock climbing, volunteering, studying new topics, and doing anything creative.

Chuck would love to hear from you and know how the concepts in this book have impacted your life. You can connect with and message him at:

https://www.linkedin.com/in/chuck-pledger/

www.ingramcontent.com/pod-product-compliance
Lightning Source LLC
Chambersburg PA
CBHW021419210526
45463CB00001B/440